D Day is Here: Dramatic News Flashes Across World

ALLIES INVADE FRANCE

Airborne Troops Land Near
Le Havre : Landing Craft

PICTORIAL CHRONICLE OF
WORLD WAR II

JAP FLEET SMASHED—

14 Major Units Sunk or Damaged: 350 Jap Pl

FORTS

3 Miles

LIGHT HOUSE

Urville
Nacqueville

Henneville
Tonneville

Ste Croix Hague

OCTEVILLE

Flotterian
ville

Bretteville

CHERBOURG

Digosville

Mesnil

NAZIS LOSE
80,000 IN ITALY

KESSELRING FACES BIG NEW BLOWS

DRIVING against the enemy on all fronts, General Alexander's troops were to-day reported to have "ironed out" all the bulges in their line, and a double drive for the important seaports of Leghorn and Ancona is now under way.

On the Adriatic coast Allied spearheads are now only 27

Mr. Hore-Belisha
Weds Heroine
of P.O.W. Camp

MR. LESLIE HORE-BELISHA, M.P., former War Minister, was married to-day at the Kingston district Registrar's Office, Norbiton, to Miss Cynthia Elliot, daughter of Mrs. Gilbert Elliot, of Portman-square, London. Miss Elliot is a cousin of Lord Minto.

Four years ago to-day Miss Elliot was captured by the Germans when serving with a canteen unit in France. For over three years she was a prisoner in

Marshalsea Road, London, S.E.1   No. 13,824   WEDNESDAY, AUGUST 14, 1940   ONE PENNY

R.A.F. WIN AGAIN—6 TO 1

57 Nazis Down In Mass Raids

WE LOSE 9 'PLANES: TWO PILOTS SAFE

THE R.A.F. won another great victory in the non-stop Channel air battle yesterday, when they shot down German raiders at the rate of six to one. Fifty-seven enemy 'planes were definitely destroyed, it was officially stated, but the total was expected to rise when full reports were received.

One More for the R.A.F. 'Bag'

Albania is at War

DUCE FAILS TO STEM REVOLT

From TERENCE ATHERTON,
Daily Mail Special Correspondent.

BELGRADE, Tuesday.

SALONIKA reports that heavy clashes are continuing between native rebels and Italians in Albania.

The rebel force, it is estimated now consists of 10,000 men operating against Italians in the Mirdiat Mati and

Raising 'Exempt' Age

By Daily Mail Political Correspondent

THE schedule of reserved occupations is being drastically revised by Mr. Ernest Bevin, the Minister of Labour.

Those who have previously been exempt from military service at 30 and over in certain occupations are likely to be liable up to 35 in the revised proposals.

ANOTHER 25 GERMAN 'PLANES SHOT DOWN

WORLD WAR II
A PICTORIAL HISTORY

DUNCAN HILL

PHOTOGRAPHS
Daily Mail

Atlantic Publishing

Published by Atlantic Publishing in 2016

Atlantic publishing
38 Copthorne Road
Croxley Green
Hertfordshire, WD3 4AQ, UK

© Atlantic Publishing
Photographs © Daily Mail Archive

A catalogue record for this book is available from the
British Library.

ISBN 978-1-909242-54-8
Printed in China

Acknowledgements

The photographs in this book are from the archives of the *Daily
Mail*. Particular thanks to Steve Torrington, Alan Pinnock, Dave
Sheppard and all the staff.

Thanks also to Alison Gauntlett, Lauren Oing, Michael Quiello,
Bradford Swann, Laurence Socha, Christopher Sullivan,
Patricia Annunziata, Caitlin Gildea, Cliff Salter, Alice Hill,
Jill Dorman and Richard Betts

Dedicated to Eric McDonald Good

Contents

THOUSANDS OF U.S. TROOPS
HAVE LANDED IN AUSTRALIA

CONVOY BEAT OFF
ALL JAP ATTACKS

A SOLDIER WITH "LOTS OF MONEY"

"UNHEALTHY INFLUENCE IN THE ARMY"

SUMMONED TO "PROVE INNOCENCE"

NEW MOVE AGAINST FOOD RACKETEERS

A.T.S. FREE

THOUSANDS OF GRADE C MEN

Share Yo

Eveniven t

Introduction

A mere 20 years after the Treaty of Versailles had, supposedly, drawn a line under 'the war to end all wars', the world was consumed by an even bloodier global conflagration. The 1919 treaty imposed swingeing terms on vanquished Germany, leaving it emasculated and humiliated; a nation seething with discontent, an economy crippled by hyper-inflation. Adolf Hitler, an Iron Cross-winning soldier in the 1914–18 conflict, was among the embittered. He blamed the Jews for all ills, and brought his warped views on racial purity into the political mainstream when his Nazi Party gained power in 1933.

Hitler dreamed of a glorious, 1000-year Reich. Territorial gains in Austria and Czechoslovakia were never going to sate his militaristic desires, a forlorn hope Britain and France still cleaved to at the beginning of 1939. Winston Churchill, then on the political sidelines, was one of the few siren voices warning of the Nazi threat. When Germany turned its expansionist gaze on Poland on 1 September 1939, war was inevitable. A vindicated Churchill emerged from his 'wilderness years' to head the Coalition Government. His stirring speeches helped boost morale, even as the German Army cut a swathe across western Europe, with Britain the final prize. The situation became even more perilous as Mussolini's Italy weighed in on the Axis side just as the Battle of Britain was about to begin in the summer of 1940.

America played a pivotal role. Its Lend-Lease arrangement kept the Allies well supplied; in the Atlantic Charter Churchill and US President Franklin Roosevelt expressed their shared principles and goals, which could only be implemented 'after the final destruction of the Nazi tyranny'; Roosevelt fully backed the Manhattan Project, America's atomic weapons programme; and following the attack on Pearl Harbor in December 1941, the Axis now had to contend with the mighty US military machine.

The Allies prevailed, and the 'broad, sunlit uplands' of victory and freedom became a reality after six years of bloodshed. The battle was won first in Europe, when the full horrors of the Nazi death camps were revealed; then in Japan, after President Truman sanctioned the use of the atomic bomb on Hiroshima and Nagasaki. The obliteration of those cities helped make this the first war to claim more civilian than servicemen's lives, over 50 million fatalities in total.

World War II: A Pictorial History uses contemporaneous reports and photographs from the *Daily Mail* archives, including many eyewitness accounts, to show how the conflict developed, describing the key battles, tactical decisions and turning points that settled the outcome.

LEFT: **In October 1942 aboard a US aircraft carrier in the Pacific, scout aircraft and dive-bombers, tightly packed together on deck, are refuelled and rearmed, ready for attack on the Japanese.**

The rise of Hitler

The end of the First World War had not really brought about any improvement in the level of tension between nations; it had simply changed the nature of the grievances and added some new ones. After the war, hopes for future peace in the world had been enshrined in the League of Nations, created to provide for a policy of 'Collective Security', but there were some doubts about how effective it would be, doubts which were to be fully vindicated.

Adolf Hitler had first come to public attention in 1923 when he made an unconstitutional attempt to seize power in Bavaria, known as the 'Munich Putsch'. It failed and he was sent to prison for nine months as a consequence.

While imprisoned, he used the time to write *Mein Kampf* (My Struggle), which became his political programme. He claimed that Germany had not really been defeated in 1918, and that both the apparent defeat and the post-war settlement had been a betrayal, for which he blamed the Jews. One of the consequences of the Munich Putsch was that Hitler was now determined to seek power by legitimate means, as far as that was possible. Following his release in 1924, he reorganized his political party, the National Socialists or Nazi party, creating what was in effect a private army. This paramilitary organization was known as the SA (Sturmabteilung), and by 1927 there were over 30,000 members. They were the 'Brownshirts', who intimidated their opponents and instigated violent conflicts with both Communists and Jews. In the meantime, the economic situation in Germany went from bad to worse.

ABOVE: **Nazi supporters line the streets of Weimar during Hitler's visit to the town in July 1936.**

RIGHT: **Crowds fawn upon Hitler as he attends Labour Day celebrations in Berlin's Lustgarten in May 1934.**

OPPOSITE LEFT: **Upon becoming Chancellor, Hitler set about consolidating his power. He had his closest rivals murdered on the 'Night of the Long Knives' in July 1934.**

OPPOSITE BELOW LEFT: **German soldiers marching at a military parade in Berlin in 1935.**

OPPOSITE BELOW MIDDLE: **Hitler addresses a crowd of Hitler Youth at the annual Nazi Party Congress in Nuremberg.**

OPPOSITE BELOW RIGHT: **German troops in Berlin swear an oath of allegiance to Adolf Hitler in 1934.**

OPPOSITE RIGHT ABOVE: **Hitler poses for a photograph with a Polish delegation led by Poland's Foreign Minister, Colonel Joseph Beck. One of Hitler's first foreign policy achievements as Chancellor was to conclude a Non-Aggression Pact with neighbouring Poland.**

The Great Depression

In October 1929, a contagious outbreak of panic selling on the New York Stock Exchange – which had previously been booming – resulted in the Wall Street Crash. This financial disaster wiped millions of dollars off the value of shares and reverberated on the global economy as a whole, ushering in the Great Depression. The economic collapse had an enormous impact throughout Europe, but was most severe in Germany, where the government was completely dependent on American finance. The value of the mark fell swiftly and catastrophically, unemployment soared and, not surprisingly, discontent spread. In this atmosphere the more moderate and democratic political parties were unable to provide any solutions to the problems besetting the nation. People began to turn to the extreme parties of the right and left in increasing numbers and unrest and violent street fighting became more common.

Nazi popularity grows

There were only 12 National Socialist members in the Reichstag, the German parliament, at the start of 1930. However, as the Great Depression set in, support for the Nazis skyrocketed. They won 107 seats in the elections of autumn 1930, becoming the second-strongest political party in the Reichstag. Hitler stood for the presidency of Germany in 1932 and won more than 13 million votes, placing him a close second behind Paul von Hindenburg, the great general of the First World War. Parliamentary elections that year saw the Nazis become the largest single party in the Reichstag. Alarmed at the rapid rise of Hitler and his party, a group of Conservative politicians persuaded President Hindenburg to appoint Hitler as Chancellor. They hoped that they could control Hitler by bringing him into the establishment and separating him from his party.

The Führer

However, the Nazis continued to expand their influence. Chancellor Hitler blamed the Communists for an arson attack on the Reichstag building in February 1933. This certainly boosted support for the Nazi party in the March 1933 elections, and allowed them to achieve an overall majority in parliament.

Hitler used his small majority to pass a law giving him power as Chancellor to govern without the consent of the Reichstag. President Hindenburg died in August 1934 and Hitler seized the opportunity to combine the two offices of the Chancellor and the President in one new role. He was now in control of the armed forces and used the title 'Führer', the leader of all the German people. All German servicemen had to swear an oath of personal loyalty to him.

Appeasement

While he consolidated his power inside Germany, Hitler moved cautiously in his foreign policy. He signed a non-aggression pact with Poland and agreed to negotiate with European powers over disarmament. However, from 1934 he secretly began rearming Germany so that it would become strong enough to achieve his main foreign policy goal: the reversal of the Treaty of Versailles.

As the 1930s progressed, the German military grew stronger and the international situation became ever more favourable. The failure of the League of Nations to tackle both Japanese aggression in Manchuria in 1931 and Italian aggression in Abyssinia in 1935 made it obvious that the organization would not seriously challenge Hitler's attempts to reverse the Treaty of Versailles. The ineffectiveness of the League revealed that the Great Powers were distracted and indifferent. The United States, Britain and France were still grappling with the Great Depression and Stalin was busy purging and collectivizing in the Soviet Union.

Reoccupying the Rhine

In 1936 Hitler decided to test the waters and send troops into the Rhineland, which had been established as a demilitarized zone under the terms of the treaty. His officers had been instructed to withdraw should they encounter any resistance. However, there was no response from the Great Powers, and an emboldened Hitler began building a line of fortifications along the French and Belgian borders.

Austria was the next country to attract his attention. The Treaty of Versailles had decreed that Austria and Germany should never be united. Austria was, however, in chaos – much of it caused by Austrian Nazis – and Hitler used this as a pretext for sending the German Army into the country. On March 13, 1938, his troops marched into Vienna and Austria was integrated into the Reich. Hitler, himself an Austrian, returned in triumph to the capital where he had lived in poverty before the First World War.

Next on Hitler's agenda was Czechoslovakia, a democratic country that had been created by the Versailles Treaty. Some three million Germans lived in Czechoslovakia, mainly in a region along the German border called the Sudetenland. Hitler insisted that this region should be absorbed into the Reich.

ABOVE RIGHT: **Hitler follows his army into Linz, Austria, to oversee the 'Anschluss', the Union of Austria and Germany, in March 1938.**

RIGHT INSET: **Neville Chamberlain returns home waving a 'piece of paper' signed by Hitler promising a peaceful resolution to European disputes in future. Chamberlain declared that he had returned bringing 'peace with honour ... peace for our time.'**

ABOVE: **American President Franklin Delano Roosevelt pictured in his home in Hyde Park, New York, in 1938. The United States stayed out of European disputes while it tried to rebuild its battered economy in the 1930s.**

BELOW: **Hitler's position was further strengthened in May 1939 when he signed an alliance, 'The Pact of Steel', with Mussolini.**

The Munich Agreement

These demands caused concern in London, but Britain was in no position to challenge Germany in Central Europe. The British military was greatly overstretched across the vast Empire and the public had no appetite for a new European conflict. Instead, British Prime Minister Neville Chamberlain went to Germany to negotiate with Hitler. At their meeting in Munich on September 29, 1938, Hitler and Chamberlain agreed that the Sudetenland should join Germany, but that this would be Hitler's last territorial demand in Europe. Chamberlain returned, claiming he had secured 'peace for our time', but his critics labelled this as 'appeasement'.

The Nazi–Soviet pact

The British government began preparing for a war during 1939 by speeding up programmes of rearmament and civil defence. However, the government's inherent anti-Communism meant that it was slow to develop ties with the Soviet Union, which were vital if Germany was to be threatened with a war on two fronts. Given the violent ideological differences between the Soviet Union and the Nazis, the British believed that Stalin would inevitably support a war against Hitler and as a consequence did very little to strengthen relations. The announcement on August 23 that Germany and the Soviet Union had signed a non-aggression pact came as a complete surprise to London. The pact was expedient; Hitler avoided a two-front war and Stalin avoided a war he was not yet ready to fight. A secret clause of the pact also promised Stalin a free hand in the Baltic states and in eastern Poland. On September 1, 1939, with his Eastern Front secure, Hitler risked war in the west by invading Poland.

ABOVE LEFT: **Hitler and Chamberlain meet at Bad Godesberg in Germany on September 23, 1938, where Hitler detailed his demands for the Sudetenland. Chamberlain spent the week convincing the Czechoslovak government to agree the terms before signing the Agreement with Hitler in Munich a week later.**

LEFT: **Hitler congratulates his Foreign Minister, Joachim von Ribbentrop, upon his return from signing the Nazi-Soviet Pact in Moscow.**

BELOW: **Hitler salutes as he walks through a sea of flowers in the Sudetenland, October 3, 1938.**

ABOVE RIGHT: **Joseph Stalin, leader of the Soviet Union, pictured at a conference in January 1938. In the late 1930s, Stalin was preoccupied with industrial development, agricultural collectivization and purging Russian society of 'saboteurs'.**

Occupation of Czechoslovakia

In March 1939, under the pretext of unrest in Slovakia, Germany occupied the rest of Czechoslovakia. However willing and able to resist Nazi aggression, Czechoslovakia would not go to war without support from Britain and France who maintained their course of appeasement. Hitler forced a bloodless surrender by Czechoslovakia and brought some of its territories under control as German Protectorates. The rest of the country was gradually broken up, with Hungary and Poland both acquiring territory. As with all his treaties and agreements, Munich was a device to buy time and to allay the suspicions of his opponents.

Although the break-up of Czechoslovakia was achieved by political means, a government in exile was formed and many Czechs fled to serve with Allied forces; an active resistance was maintained throughout the war, notably assassinating Reinhard Heydrich, Himmler's deputy and at the time the Protector of Bohemia and Moravia.

The Munich Agreement was in tatters and the British public were outraged. Hitherto, many people had believed that Hitler's demands had been reasonable, but overt aggression in Czechoslovakia was a step too far, and the public called for firm action. In response, the British government issued guarantees to protect Poland, Romania and Greece against German aggression.

ABOVE: **A local girl in the newly 'freed' Sudeten areas fraternises with German soldiers after troops occupied the No.2 zone of the Czech Sudetenland in October 1938, in accordance with the recently agreed Four Power Pact.**

BELOW: **The inhabitants give a hearty welcome to German troops at Kleinphilipsreuth.**

OPPOSITE ABOVE: **Crestfallen men and women watch the Germans troops enter Prague on March 17, 1939.**

OPPOSITE BELOW: **An elderly lady in Friedland presents German soldiers with flowers after General Von Bock's troops crossed the Czech frontier at Rumburg and Friedland.**

DAILY MAIL   APRIL 1, 1939

British pledge to Poland is without reserve

The pledge: ... In the event of any action which clearly threatened Polish independence, and which the Polish Government accordingly considered it vital to resist with their national forces, His Majesty's Government would feel themselves bound at once to lend the Polish Government all support in their power. - The Premier in the House yesterday.

Britain has offered Poland a mutual anti-aggression pact to which other Powers will be invited to subscribe. It is hoped that Col. Beck, Polish Foreign Minister, will sign it when he comes to London next week. The pledge given by the Prime Minister in the House of Commons yesterday to support Poland if she is attacked was purely to cover an interim period following rumours - which have not been confirmed - of German troop movements.

Apparently the Cabinet thought that the situation in Eastern Europe was sufficiently urgent to justify a unilateral declaration by the British Government. Ministers were also becoming acutely aware of the necessity to give the country some idea of their intentions.

The pledge given by the Prime Minister goes far beyond any commitment entered into by Britain since the end of the Great War. It is meant to form the basis of a strong anti-aggression front, by which it is hoped to preserve peace.

The Prime Minister's pledge to Poland is without reservation. Contrary to assertions made in London yesterday, there are no British conditions regarding Danzig or the Polish Corridor.

BRITAIN & FRANCE AT WAR WITH GERMANY

We meet a challenge which would be fatal to civilisation

The King's Message

Poles Launch Counter-attack

POLES SM
INTO EAS

German invasion of Poland

In the early hours of September 1, 1939, German troops crossed the border into Polish territory, triggering the largest war the world has ever seen. The Polish Army, consisting mainly of cavalry divisions, was no match for the modern, mechanized German Army. The Luftwaffe quickly won air superiority over the smaller Polish Air Force and began pummelling Polish cities. As Poland met its fate, frantic debates ensued in London and Paris over how to respond. By evening, the decision was made to issue an ultimatum demanding that Hitler withdraw promptly from Poland or face war.

The British and French Ambassadors handed the text of their ultimatums to the German foreign minister, Ribbentrop, who agreed to pass them on to Hitler. The British and French ultimatums expired at 11 am and 5 pm respectively on Sunday, September 3. Neither country received a reply from Hitler and consequently a state of war ensued.

DAILY MAIL SEPTEMBER 4, 1939

War 11a.m., September 3, 1939

Great Britain and France are at war with Germany. We now fight against the blackest tyranny that has ever held men in bondage. We fight to defend, and to restore, freedom and justice on earth.

Let us face the truth. This was inevitable whether it began with Austria, Sudetenland, Bohemia, or Danzig. If it had not come over Danzig it would have come later upon some other issue. It became inevitable from the day Hitler seized power in Germany and began his criminal career by enslaving his own people. For his one aim since then has been gradually to enslave all others by the methods of brute force.

Once more Britain, her Empire and her friends are engaged in a conflict to uphold Right against Might.

If the democracies had flinched now, they would have been compelled to abdicate for ever their title to be called the champions of liberty. The fate of these small nations who have already lost their rights would have been theirs in turn.

This was the dominant thought in the inspiring message broadcast by the King to his people last night. We go to war because we must. In His Majesty's words: 'For the sake of all that we ourselves hold dear, and of the world's order and peace, it is unthinkable that we should refuse to meet the challenge.'

BELOW: Hitler addresses the Reichstag in the Kroll Opera House on the day of the invasion of Poland. In the speech he blamed Poland for starting the war by firing upon German territory that morning. He warned that 'whoever departs from the rules of humane warfare can only expect that we shall do the same'.

ABOVE: Polish refugees stream out of Warsaw to escape the relentless bombardment.

LEFT: Poles march through Warsaw on their way to dig trenches for the defence of the city.

Stalin invades Poland

The Polish commander, Marshal Rydz-Smigly, hoped in vain that Polish defences could hold out until Britain and France attacked in the west. However, his men were sitting ducks for Germany's 'Stuka' dive-bombers, and Polish cavalrymen were gunned down with ease as they futilely tried to take on German tank units.

On September 17, Stalin moved his troops into eastern Poland to fulfil the secret clause of the Nazi-Soviet Pact. He disguised his land grab as a mission to liberate Ukrainians and White Russians from Polish domination. The Red Army encountered little resistance from the Poles who were completely tied up on the Western Front. On September 28, Ribbentrop met with his Soviet counterpart Vyacheslav Molotov to sign the German-Soviet Boundary and Friendship Treaty, which officially carved up Poland between them. There was some resentment among Germans that the Soviets were to be handed territory that had been won by the Wehrmacht, especially as Stalin waited more than two weeks before declaring war.

The fall of Warsaw

The Polish capital, Warsaw, held out for several weeks against the Wehrmacht, which feared that street fighting would be too costly. Instead, the German Army besieged the city and then bombed it into submission. The devastating attacks resulted in thousands of civilian deaths and the destruction of the city. The troops defending Warsaw surrendered on September 27 in order to relieve the suffering of the civilian population, but the German occupation that followed was to make their lives much worse. Politicians, academics, soldiers and ordinary civilians were massacred as the Nazis immediately set about destroying any potential opposition. The Germans began to ethnically cleanse Poland by expelling the 'subhuman' Poles from their homes and sending German families to replace them. Exceptions were made for those who were deemed sufficiently Aryan and agreed to be 'Germanized'.

Polish Jews were singled out for the harshest treatment; they were subjected to barbaric attacks and forced to move to ghettos, cut off from the outside world. However, this was to be a temporary arrangement, and Poland's Jewish population was to suffer an even worse fate when the Nazis decided upon their 'Final Solution'.

*ABOVE: **Hitler observes the destruction of Warsaw from a hill overlooking the city.***

*ABOVE LEFT: **Polish POWs line up for food in German prison camps.***

*LEFT: **German troops train in preparation for air raids after the Allied declaration of war.***

*BELOW: **Polish troops wait for the Germans to arrive in Warsaw after the city's capitulation.***

The Evening News

LARGEST EVENING NET SALE IN THE WORLD

POLAND INVADED

Big German Offensive on the Corridor : Bombing Raids on Warsaw, Cracow and other Polish Towns

DANZIG ANNEXED TO-DAY BY PROCLAMATION

French Cabinet Met and Issued Order For General Mobilisation

HITLER AND ITALY: "I DO NOT APPEAL TO FOREIGN HELP"

PARLIAMENT SUMMONED FOR 6 P.M.

BRITAIN STANDS BY POLAND

19 Tube Stations To Close

Hitler—"Goering Is My Successor If I Fall"

Britain prepares for war

In Britain and France there seemed to be little change in the months immediately following the declaration of war. In Britain rationing began. A night-time blackout was introduced and children were evacuated from cities to the country – both measures designed to protect the country from German air raids, which were not to happen for another nine months. There were, however, some raids on shipping by German submarines. A large French Army and a much smaller British Expeditionary Force maintained defensive positions in northern France, preparing for the possibility of invasion. As the months passed, it seemed increasingly unlikely that Hitler would strike in western Europe, and talk of a 'phoney war' spread. Further to the east, the situation was different: bitter fighting continued in Poland, Lithuania, Latvia and Estonia.

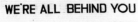

To Chamberlain:-
KILL NAZISM FOR EVER
WE'RE ALL BEHIND YOU

LEFT: Shop signs supporting the government's declaration of war against the Nazi regime became commonplace.

BELOW: The statue of Eros in Piccadilly Circus, London, is boarded up to protect it from the impending air raids.

TOP: Troops marching into Piccadilly Circus in 1939. Little funding had been made available for the military during the 1920s and 1930s and rearmament and civil defence programmes had to be rapidly stepped up after the Sudetenland crisis in 1938.

ABOVE: Children are taught how to use gas masks. The British government feared Germany would mount a gas attack and implored people to 'always carry your gas mask'. In the event, poison gas was never used during air raids on Britain.

DIG FOR VICTORY

HITLER INVADES NORWAY AND DENMARK

ALLIES TO TAKE ACTION FORTHWITH

War in Scandinavia

At the end of 1939 the Red Army invaded neutral Finland because the Finnish government had refused to accept Stalin's territorial demands. Helsinki was badly damaged by Soviet bombing raids, but the winter snow came to the aid of the Finns. Finnish soldiers used guerrilla tactics to slow and reverse the Soviet advance during December and January. The Soviets struck back with a major offensive in February, forcing the Finnish government to accept a punitive peace agreement.

On April 9,1940, Hitler launched simultaneous attacks against major ports in Denmark and Norway. There were some contingents from Britain and its Allies already in Norway, and these were rapidly deployed in defence. But the German command of the air – and a general lack of reinforcements, despite strong naval support – meant that the defenders were quickly forced to withdraw. However, the Allies were successful in managing to inflict significant losses on the German fleet during the Norwegian campaign.

ABOVE: Iron railings were removed from many British public places such as parks, gardens and squares in order to be smelted for use in munitions. Private owners were encouraged to do the same.

FAR LEFT: Signposts and street names were removed across Britain in case they assisted invading German troops.

LEFT: British Boy Scouts collect waste paper as the country embarked on a recycling drive.

BELOW: Sandbags being filled in Hampstead. They were used to protect buildings across the country.

Evacuating the cities

As the most likely targets of German bombing raids, London and other major British industrial cities began to see the mass evacuation of schoolchildren to rural areas from September 1939. For many children it would be the first time they had been separated from their families, and would certainly be the first time that most would spend Christmas in unfamiliar surroundings.

BELOW: **Carrying their gas masks in cases and wearing luggage labels to help identify them, this group of children from the Hugh Myddelton School in Clerkenwell were part of the first wave of evacuees who left London on the day Hitler invaded Poland, September 1, 1939.**

BOTTOM RIGHT: **Children at Maryville Road School in Leyton, London, are escorted into the school air raid shelter for safety. The start of term had been delayed by many weeks, as schools could not reopen until they had their own air raid shelter. Schools were only allowed to teach the number of children** the shelter could accommodate, often resulting in a part-time shift system with many pupils limited to half a day's schooling.

BELOW RIGHT: **A group of young children sheltering during an air raid at a school on the south coast; teachers used songs and comics to entertain them.**

DAILY MAIL   SEPTEMBER 2, 1939

'The children have all behaved marvellously'

The greatest organised movement of a human population in the world's history started yesterday. As if by some quiet smooth-working machine, nearly 1,000,000 children, mothers, blind and maimed people were taken from danger to safety. In three days – perhaps less – 3,000,000 will have made the journey across the invisible frontier. Thousands of households all over Britain yesterday welcomed small strangers who were to be for a time members of the family.

Most homes in the evacuated areas were adapting themselves bravely to a sadder change which had robbed them of their children. London has lost much of its laughter. Nearly half of the 3,000,000 are being evacuated from the Greater London area. The rest are from the naval and shipping areas and the industrial districts of the Midlands, North, and Scotland.

Everywhere the task of moving this enormous number of children was carried out with great ease, owing to the thorough preparation and the co-operation of officials, parents, and children. And officials everywhere said 'the children behaved simply marvellously.'

Seeking safety

In the first weeks of the war nearly four million people moved from evacuation centres to reception areas. These included pregnant women, mothers of pre-school children and disabled people, as well as school-age children. Throughout the war, evacuation schemes continued, with peak numbers related directly to the severity of the bombing. After the 'phoney war' of the first year, many children returned home, only to be re-evacuated when the Blitz began. Even before then, some children, evacuated to the south coast of England, had to be relocated when the area suffered attacks during the summer of 1940.

School-age children were evacuated without their parents. They were required to report to their school with only a change of clothes, basic toilet essentials, a packed lunch and, of course, a gas mask. At the school they were tagged with luggage labels, a precaution against children becoming lost but especially important for the youngest, who may not have known their address. Accompanied by teachers and helpers, the children were taken by buses and trains to the reception areas. Trips were as long as twelve hours; many children arrived exhausted by the journey, upset at leaving their parents and fearful of what life would be like in their new home.

TOP: **Initially, those who had been evacuated to coastal areas were able to enjoy their freedom, playing on the beaches. This activity was limited as gradually coastlines were covered in barbed wire to protect the public from mines, which had been laid to prevent the enemy landing.**

RIGHT: **Even prior to the declaration of war, children began to be evacuated from areas most at risk of bombing. These schoolchildren from Edgware, London, were ferried by buses to the railway station.**

BELOW: **A group of British children wave goodbye to their families as they wait to board a train.**

Recruiting a fighting force

Following the declaration of war there was an immediate need to increase the number of men in the British armed services. In May 1939 a very limited conscription bill was introduced. However, on the outbreak of war, parliament passed the National Service (Armed Forces) Act which meant that men between the ages of 18 and 41 could be called upon to join up unless rejected on medical grounds or working in a 'reserved' occupation – a civilian job considered vital to the war effort. By 1942 the perameters were widened to include men aged between 18 and 51 and unmarried women and widows without children between the ages of 20 and 30.

TOP: Soon after the evacuation from Dunkirk, on June 22, 1940, 30,000 men registered for military service at Labour Exchanges throughout the country.

MIDDLE: Charles Remnant calls for volunteers to join the 'Citizen's Army' at a meeting held on Tooting Bec Common in South London.

BELOW: The first batch of men aged 22, but not yet 23, report to various military centres for training, January 15, 1940.

Defenders of the home front

Although its appeasement strategy prevailed until Germany's invasion of Poland, Britain had been preparing for possible war. The consequences of the German incursion into Poland could be seen immediately as Polish resistance rapidly failed and in response to fears of an invasion of Britain, Churchill proposed the formation of a defence force of 500,000 volunteers not deemed fit for military service but still able to fight. On May 14, 1940, Anthony Eden, Secretary of State for War, broadcast to the nation inviting men to sign up for the Local Defence Volunteers. The bland acronym LDV and the problems of training and equipment held back its success. Churchill turned the situation around by renaming it the Home Guard in July.

The Battle of Britain and the threatened German invasion made the Home Guard one more demand among many for training and equipment; the return from Dunkirk of thousands of troops minus their weapons made those combatants a priority and the role of the Home Guard was seen as secondary support. However by 1943, although the threat of invasion had largely subsided, the Home Guard was more of a force to be reckoned with, numbering 1.5 million, armed and trained, with a plan of defence – from standing look-out for German paratroop attacks, to guerrilla warfare. The Home Guard was stood down in December 1944, finally disbanding in December 1945.

TOP: **Local Defence Volunteers (LDV) on parade. The LDV was set up as Germany unleashed its blitzkrieg in Europe. In July 1940 the LDV changed its name to the Home Guard, which later became affectionately known as 'Dad's Army'. Many of those who joined up were older but had seen action in the Great War.**

ABOVE: **Local Defence Volunteers march at a parade ground in Balham. They are weaponless but some have LDV armbands and soldiers' caps.**

BELOW: **Men parade on Tooting Bec Common, dressed in civilian clothes and 'armed' with sticks and umbrellas.**

DAILY MAIL   SEPTEMBER 12, 1939
Britain's troops in action on western front – official

British troops have landed in France and are in action alongside the French Army. They have taken part in the advances into German territory. This news was released dramatically at 9.35 p.m. yesterday by the Ministry of Information.

The transport of the B.E.F. has taken several days, and has been carried out successfully without the loss of a single life.

The despatch of the troops was carried out with the greatest secrecy, so as to reduce to a minimum the danger of attack by submarines or aircraft. A tremendous ovation was given by the French populace when the first soldier marched ashore - and the scenes recalled those of 1914. No details of the units or their positions in France can be given.

The fall of France

Just before dawn on May 10, 1940, the German assault on western Europe finally began. In a swift and comprehensive move, soon to be widely known as blitzkrieg, German paratroopers and bombers successfully struck at positions in Holland, Belgium and Luxembourg, facilitating rapid infantry assaults deep into these countries. In response, the Allies committed a large part of their forces to Belgium.

The German troops advanced at speed through the Low Countries, aiming to cut the Allied forces in two and push many of their troops towards the coast. At the same time armoured Panzer divisions broke through the French lines at Sedan. They stormed across northern France, heading towards the Channel coast within a matter of days. There was comparative chaos in the Allied forces; the speed and scope of the assault had stunned everyone. Their troops in the north, now caught in the German pincer movement, began to retreat towards the Channel ports, notably to a perimeter line around Dunkirk. A huge evacuation from France was authorized on May 26. This evacuation would be the first test for Winston Churchill, who had replaced Neville Chamberlain as Britain's Prime Minister sixteen days earlier; Chamberlain had finally resigned following severe criticism over the government's response to the German advances in Norway and Denmark.

TOP: French soldiers march towards the front line. Germany unexpectedly invaded France through the dense forest of the Ardennes region of Belgium, and in doing so, circumvented France's heavily defended 'Maginot Line' fortifications along the German border.

ABOVE: French troops take aim at German positions from the first-floor windows of a ruined house in a village near the Belgian border. The French military censor forbade the publication of the name of the village.

BELOW: With fierce fighting occurring on the other side of the building, French troops run from house to house to take up more positions in a desperate attempt to stem the German advance until reinforcements arrive.

LEFT: More troops rush up a rickety stairway to man the first-floor windows, while their commanding officer issues orders from a niche in the wall in the right of the picture.

335,000 SAVED FROM DUNKIRK
Mr. Churchill On Glorious Feat By 1,000 Ships

Dunkirk

In the event, the evacuation, codenamed Operation Dynamo, was an enormous success. It had been thought that some 45,000 Allied troops could be rescued from Dunkirk – but 338,226 men were recovered from the beaches between May 26 and June 4, in often appalling conditions. There were many naval ships, but the evacuation was marked by the use of hundreds of small ships – whatever vessels were available on the south coast of Britain. The weather, by and large, was favourable and the RAF were also able to help, but the evacuation beaches were under almost constant attack. Dynamo was a success in terms of the number of lives saved, but thousands of vehicles, weapons and tons of supplies were left behind.

The Vichy government

Hitler had succeeded in gaining control of the Channel coast, and the rest of France was soon to fall. The German Army entered Paris some ten days later, on June 14 – just a month after the initial attacks on the country. Italy entered the war in support of Hitler and, by June 22, 1940, with all of northern France occupied by German troops and columns advancing southwards towards the border with Spain, the French Premier, Marshal Pétain, agreed to an armistice with Hitler. Under its conditions, France had to disarm and was to be divided into two sections. The northern zone and the northern and western coasts were under direct German control, but the southern part of the country would be governed by a collaborationist government led by Pétain and based at the spa town of Vichy. By the end of June the British-owned Channel Islands, so close to France, had also fallen to Germany.

TOP LEFT: **French tanks on manoeuvres in January 1940.** This period was known as the 'Phoney War' because both sides had declared a state of war existed, but neither side had launched an attack.

UPPER MIDDLE LEFT: **French soldiers return from manning border posts during the 'Phoney War' period.**

LOWER MIDDLE LEFT: **Reservists dig air-raid shelters in Paris in September 1939.**

BOTTOM LEFT: **Paris experiences its first air raid, September 1939.** There was relatively little aerial bombardment of the city in comparison with other European capitals.

TOP: **Columns of Allied soldiers await evacuation from the beach at Dunkirk.**

R.A.F. WIN AGAIN—6 TO 1

57 Nazis Down In Mass Raids

WE LOSE 9 'PLANES: TWO PILOTS SAFE

One More for the R.A.F. 'Bag'

Albania is at War

DUCE FAILS TO STEM REVOLT

From TERENCE ATHERTON, Daily Mail Special Correspondent.

Raising 'Exempt' Age

By Daily Mail Political Correspondent

THE schedule of reserved occupations is being drastically revised by Mr. Ernest Bevin, the Minister of Labour.

...se who have previous... exempt from milita... e at 30 and over in ce... ccupations are likely ...le up to 35 in the ...als.

...Bevin hopes to be able ...e the revised sched... ...n the next provision... ...f further classes

The Battle of Britain

Most of western Europe was now under Hitler's control, but Britain remained a serious obstacle to his ambitions. He set his sights on invading the country, developing a plan called Operation Sea Lion. In order for this to be successful, however, Germany had to control the Channel and subdue Britain's south coast. As a result, attacks were initiated both on the sea and from the air. Shipping convoys were the first victims and then, by August 1940, attacks began on the vital airfields of southern England. This was the start of the Battle of Britain.

ABOVE LEFT: **An aerial view of the Luftwaffe flying over Britain.**

TOP RIGHT: **A German plane plummets to the ground over Sussex in August 1940.**

LEFT: **Squadron Leader Douglas Bader had a distinguished career as an RAF pilot, despite having lost both of his legs in a crash in 1931.**

ABOVE: **Britain's new Prime Minister, Winston Churchill, visits Ramsgate, one of the most heavily affected areas of Britain during the Battle of Britain in 1940.**

BELOW: A squadron of Hurricane fighters fly in close formation. Along with the Spitfire this aircraft was the best defence Britain had against the Luftwaffe.

TOP RIGHT: Much of the Battle of Britain was confined to the south east of England. However, German fighters menaced the skies all over the country. This reconnaissance plane was brought down in Scotland.

MIDDLE RIGHT: Vapour trails mark the scene of a dogfight between the RAF and the Luftwaffe. Curious civilians often came onto the streets to watch and cheer on the RAF.

BOTTOM RIGHT: Bren gunners keep a watchful eye on the skies over Britain.

DAILY MAIL JUNE 19, 1940

The Battle of Britain

The Prime Minister gave the House of Commons last night 'some indication of the solid, practical grounds upon which we are basing our invincible resolve to continue the war.'

The professional advisers of the three Services, he said, unitedly advised that we should do it and that there were good and reasonable hopes of final victory.

In this island there were now over 1,250,000 men under arms, backed by 500,000 Local Defence Volunteers. We might expect very large additions to our weapons in the near future. And, 'after all we have a Navy, which some people seem to forget.' Our fighter air strength is stronger at present in relation to Germany's than it had ever been.

'The Battle of Britain' said Mr. Churchill, 'is about to begin. On this battle depends the survival of Christian civilisation. I look forward confidently to the exploits of our fighter pilots, who will have the glory of saving their native land and our island home from the most deadly of all attacks.

'There remains the danger of the bombing attacks, which will certainly be made very soon upon us by the bomber forces of the enemy. It is quite true that these forces are superior in number to ours, but we have a very large bombing force also, which we shall use to strike at the military targets in Germany without intermission.

'What General Weygand called the Battle of France is over. The Battle of Britain is about to begin. On this battle depends the survival of Christian civilisation. Upon it depends our own British life and the long continuity of our institutions and our Empire. The whole fury and might of the enemy must very soon be turned upon us. Hitler knows he will have to break us in this island or lose the war. If we can stand up to him all Europe may be freed and the life of the world may move forward into broad, sunlit uplands. But if we fail, the whole world, including the United States and all that we have known and cared for, will sink into the abyss of a new dark age made more sinister and perhaps more prolonged by the lights of a perverted silence.

'Let us therefore brace ourselves to our duty and so bear ourselves that if the British Commonwealth and Empire last for a thousand years, men will still say, 'This was their finest hour.'

400 Miles

LONDON RAIDERS Under a

THE London skyline silhouetted against the glare of fires started by the German bombers during their night attack on the city, and (below)

Goering's four-day promise

Hitler and his blitzkrieg commanders were understandably confident about their war machine but Nazi hubris bred false assumptions that would lead to Germany's unexpected defeat in the Battle of Britain. The Luftwaffe had dominated the skies of western Europe during the blitzkrieg; its task now was to crush the RAF and disable its aircraft production. Field Marshal Hermann Goering, the Luftwaffe commander, boasted that the RAF would be broken in four days and its production capability wiped out in four weeks. However, the RAF were not to succumb to Goering's plan; the Battle of Britain was to have four clear phases and on June 18, Churchill predicted Britain's struggle for survival with his famous 'Finest Hour' speech.

LEFT: **RAF pilots relax in their rest room at their base 'somewhere in Scotland'.**

BELOW: **Fighter pilots leap into action and rush to their planes after a warning from HQ that an unidentified plane had been spotted by the Observer Corps.**

Heavy German losses

The summer of 1940 was balmy, with many days of sunshine. Aircrews fighting for their lives one moment could be recuperating at the margins of their grassy runways soon after, ready at an instant to return to battle. However, the weather wasn't good the whole time. At the beginning of August, Eagle Day – the day the Luftwaffe planned to begin its real assault on the RAF – was quite seriously delayed by bad flying conditions, finally launching in earnest on August 13, after low cloud cleared in the early afternoon. Confusion in the German command made the planned attack less effective; the Luftwaffe were surprised by the firm resolve and force of the defending RAF who lost 13 aircraft in the air compared with 47 German planes.

DAILY MAIL   JUNE 11, 1940
Italy: hostilities open

Hostilities between Italy and the Allies began at midnight. New York reports that Italian troops invaded the French Riviera at 6.30 last night were emphatically denied by a Government spokesman in Rome.

Signor Mussolini has chosen the crucial hour in the great battle for France to take his momentous step, but Britain and France have long been prepared to meet such a situation. It can be assumed that Britain will quickly take the offensive at sea. Her naval dispositions in the Mediterranean and other preparations have been made with the object of aiming swift and heavy blows at Italy.

A few days ago the British Government, in agreement with the French, decided to impose the full force of contraband control on all Italian ships. Italian shipping at Malta was seized early this morning. All Italians on the island were rounded up.

Rome radio announced that Signor Mussolini will be Supreme Commander of Italian armed forces, "although the King of Italy still remains the nominal chief." Marshal Badoglio has been made Commander-in-Chief of the Army.

Mr. Churchill will make a statement on the new situation to-day.

TOP LEFT: **The overwhelming speed of the German war machine as it moved west, and Prime Minister Chamberlain's general failure to effect any resistance, frustrated Winston Churchill. In the years before the war, Churchill was critical of Chamberlain's lack of preparation against the obvious rearming of Germany by Hitler's Nazis. On May 10, 1940, Chamberlain resigned and recommended Churchill as** the man to head an all-party war government. Churchill accepted the invitation from King George VI and immediately stepped into the role, much to the relief of the nation. On May 13 his first great speech to Parliament, containing the immortal words 'I have nothing to offer but blood, toil, tears and sweat', was broadcast across the nation.

ABOVE: **Adolf Hitler in conference with Reichsmarschall Hermann Goering (2nd left), commander of the Luftwaffe. Hitler made him personally responsible for defeating the RAF prior to Operation Sealion, the planned invasion of Britain in September 1940.**

TOP RIGHT: **In April 1940 Winston Churchill paid a visit to one of Britain's dockyards, the primary targets for Luftwaffe bombers. Addressing the assembled workers, he asked, 'Are we downhearted?' to be greeted with a resounding, 'No!' This was a catchphrase from a song that was used throughout the Battle of Britain and the Blitz.**

Non-stop production lines

The Ministry of Aircraft Production was one of the specialized supply ministries set up by the British government during the war. As the name suggests, it was responsible for aircraft production for the British forces; primarily the Royal Air Force, but also the Fleet Air Arm. The department was formed in 1940 by Winston Churchill in response to the production problems that winning the Battle of Britain posed. The first minister was Lord Beaverbrook and under his control the Ministry presided over an enormous increase in production. Lord Beaverbrook pushed for the manufacture of aircraft to have priority over virtually all other types of munitions production when drawing on raw materials. In 1940 Britain manufactured in excess of 15,000 aircraft, 4,000 more than Germany.

LEFT: **A production line for the Miles Master, one of the RAF training aircraft.**

BELOW: **A Spitfire production line. While the Hurricane was more numerous, and accounted for more German losses than the Spitfire, the speed and agility of the Spitfire made it a formidable fighter plane.**

ABOVE: **The limitations of the Bristol Blenheim led to the development of the Beaufort, which entered service with a Coastal Command Squadron in 1940. Just over 2,000 were built, with the bulk of production at Blackburn's Yorkshire works. The light bomber was intended to carry torpedoes to be used against the German navy and in aerial mine-laying as well as in short-range sorties.**

LEFT: **The Spitfire, designed by RJ Mitchell and powered by a single Rolls-Royce engine, could fly at high or low altitudes, was able to evade most enemy fighters and also performed valuable reconnaissance work. During the war, 'Spitfire Funds' were set up, when groups would fundraise for a Spitfire to be manufactured. This was combined with public collections of donated metal such as aluminium pans. By the close of the war more than 20,000 Spitfires had been produced for the RAF.**

CHURCHILL WARNS BRITAIN AGAINST INVASION

"Next Two Weeks Are Crucial"

R.A.F. SHOWER BOMBS ON NAZI BARGE FLEET

FAR LEFT: Among the most outstanding RAF pilots during the Battle of Britain was James 'Ginger' Lacey, who shot down more German planes than any other pilot, with a total of 28 destroyed.

LEFT: Bader (centre), having just received the DSO, pictured with Pilot Officer WL McKnight (left) and Flight Lieutenant GE Ball.

BELOW: Bader (centre) surrounded by fellow officers and crew. In 1941 he had to bail out over German-occupied France and was sent to a prisoner-of-war camp. After repeated attempts to escape he was transferred to Colditz and was finally freed by the US Army in April 1945. Despite his request, he was not able to fight for the remainder of the war.

Hitler abandons 'Operation Sealion'

On September 7, the new German approach ushered in the fourth and final phase of the Battle of Britain with the beginning of the Blitz, as 950 German aircraft attacked London in the first and last massed daylight raid on the capital; 300 civilians were killed and 1,300 seriously wounded. For the next 57 consecutive days London was remorselessly bombed in night raids. Fighter Command was amazed at this change of tactics, which perversely saved it from destruction, allowing its forces to recuperate and airfields to be restored. However, it was a terrible price for Londoners to pay, the death toll rose to 2,000 by September 10. September 15 marked the heaviest bombardment of the capital so far – but at a cost to the Luftwaffe of 56 planes. This date, originally designated as the launch for 'Operation Sealion', the invasion of Britain, would prove a turning point in the Battle of Britain, as the German High Command realized that their invasion of Britain would be at an unsustainable cost. On September 17, Hitler abandoned 'Operation Sealion'; but it was not until October 29 that could Britain breathe a little easier, as the stream of German raiding aircraft subsided.

LEFT: Shipping and submarine movements are tracked in the control room of RAF Coastal Command, which provided aerial protection of Allied shipping from both the Luftwaffe and German U-boats. It received much less glory than its Fighter and Bomber Command cousins. In the first phase of the Battle of Britain, the so-called 'Kanalkampf', Luftwaffe attacks from July 10 to August 11 focused on shipping in the English Channel and the North Sea.

ABOVE: Members of the Women's Auxiliary Air Force (WAAF) in training. Although women did not fly combat missions, the contribution of women in the auxiliary services was invaluable. The WAAF staffed radar stations while, among other duties, the women in the ATS manned anti-aircraft guns. Those of the Air Transport Auxiliary flew missions delivering new aircraft.

BELOW: Women of the Auxiliary Territorial Service (ATS) on observation duty at an anti-aircraft battery. Although they didn't handle the armament they were trained to use the rangefinders and accurately identify enemy aircraft.

Counting the cost

The milestone date for the end of the Battle of Britain – October 31, 1940 – was arbitrary to some extent as Britain would continue to experience the German Blitz until early in the summer of 1941. Nevertheless, at this point in the war, it was possible to begin counting the cost of this decisive battle: during the Battle of Britain from July 10 to October 31, Britain lost 1,065 aircraft (including 1,004 fighters) and 544 fighter pilots; German losses numbered 1,922 aircraft (including 879 fighters, 80 Stukas and 881 bombers). British civilian losses in the Blitz that ended in May 1941 soared to over 40,000 killed and 50,000 injured. German Luftwaffe losses from August 1940 until March 1941 were nearly 3,000 aircraft lost and 3,363 aircrew killed, with 2,117 wounded and 2,641 taken prisoner.

BELOW: As this picture shows, RAF pilots needed considerable stamina: sorties might begin at dawn with an adrenalin-fuelled run to their aircraft, laden down with their flying equipment. At the peak of the Battle, they would continue flying sorties as long as they could keep awake and had an airworthy machine. They were known to bale out of a doomed plane, be picked up and then immediately return to combat. Many in their crippled aircraft preferred to glide to earth in forced landings, especially when over the Channel.

RIGHT: Only one member of the four-man crew of this Heinkel bomber survived when it was brought down on a night mission at the beginning of September.

DAILY MAIL   AUGUST 16, 1940

London's First Air Raid

German dive-bombers swooped on Croydon Aerodrome last evening in the first bombing raid in the London area. One bomb hit an aerodrome building and there were some casualties, but there was little damage in the town. At least one 'plane, swooping over the streets, machine-gunned groups of civilians, but there were no serious casualties.

It was London's first real air raid, and the fifth alarm of the war. Sirens were sounded all over London, the alarm lasting for only a few minutes.

Heinkel twin-engined bombers, escorted by Messerschmitt fighters, came over and divided into two sections to attack. They were met by terrific anti-aircraft gun barrage, and fighters went up to intercept them.

At least three Germans were brought down over and around Croydon, and others were destroyed on their way home. One came down in a wood and was burned out. One of the crew, caught in a tree by his parachute ropes, shook hands with his captors when released.

Several 'planes swooped to within a few hundred feet of the streets and machine-gunned civilians. A Mr. Green and his wife and children were machine-gunned as they ran to their garden shelter, but none was hit. Mrs. Green had her baby in her arms.

ABOVE LEFT: **The kills tally on this shot-down Bf 109 gives an indication of RAF losses and the performance of the German fighter plane. In the early days of the war the Bf 109 clearly had an advantage over the British machines, especially the many outdated craft that were deployed in France.**

ABOVE: **The stove in this airmen's mess provides the warming focal** point for the pilots. Their inertia belies the squadron's energy - they had a tally of 60 Luftwaffe kills by the end of 1940.

TOP: **Battle of Britain aircraft flew at great height with unpressurised cabins. From 16,000 feet oxygen was required to maintain consciousness, the cockpit would become very cold and ice could impair the** mechanics and cloud the plexiglass. To combat the intense cold, the parachute manufacturer Leslie Irvin devised the characteristic airman's jacket from very supple sheepskin, tailored to give maximum warmth while allowing freedom to move. The aircrew also wore fleece-lined boots and gloves.

Blitz on Britain's cities

Even though the invasion of Britain was called off, Germany continued to bomb Britain's cities in the hope of breaking civilian morale. The Blitz began in September 1940 with attacks on London. Civilian targets were struck across the city from the docklands in the east to Buckingham Palace in the west. Londoners were especially vulnerable because few people had space for air-raid shelters. Consequently many people crammed into underground Tube stations. These undoubtedly saved many lives, but were not without risk. On October 14, 1940, sixty-four people were killed at Balham Tube station when a bomb hit a water main, flooding the station.

Britain had been prepared for such an aerial bombardment since the beginning of the war, and many targets had been anticipated. The country had made provision for air raids: blackout conditions were imposed at night, air-raid shelters had been built, and there had even been a mass issue of gas masks, on the assumption that Hitler might make use of chemical weapons. Although poison gas was never used in the Blitz, casualties were high as densely populated areas were subjected to sustained bombardment. Though a lot of children had been evacuated to the countryside from the cities at the start of the war, most of them had returned during the period of the 'phoney war', and many of them died.

ABOVE RIGHT: **Civilians shelter during an overnight air raid in the relative safety of Holborn Tube station. Few people in London had space at their homes for an air-raid shelter, so many crowded into Underground stations. The government assisted them by putting bunkbeds and latrines in the shelters.**

ABOVE: **An anti-aircraft battery at work during a raid on the north of England.**

RIGHT: **A tramcar destroyed during a daylight raid in Blackfriars Road.**

BELOW: St Paul's Cathedral stands shrouded in smoke after a major air raid on London on Sunday December 29, 1940.

First strikes

London was the focus for most Blitz attacks. At first, the Germans mounted sorties day and night but losses were large and after a week the Luftwaffe switched most of their operations to take place under cover of darkness.

LEFT: **On the fifth night of the Blitz, East Enders used Liverpool Street and other underground stations to try to escape the bombing raids**

BELOW: **A British soldier, heavily laden with equipment, pauses for a mug of tea at a London station.**

BELOW LEFT: **Urban bombing destroyed hundreds of homes and businesses, leaving many civilians homeless and shops and services wiped out. However, people had little choice but to adjust to these challenging circumstances and most did so well. Provisions were made for the homeless, with buildings such as schools being used as temporary accomodation.**

LEFT: **Temporary Post Offices were designed to be portable and could be erected swiftly in order to replace Post Offices which had been damaged by bombing.**

ABOVE: **Women and children queue for food at a communal cooking centre set up by the London Council.**

BELOW: **This street fruit seller boasts that his oranges have come through Musso's (Mussolini's) 'Lake' – a nickname for the Mediterranean. He also has bananas for sale – a rarity during the war, especially by the time of the Blitz.**

HITLERS' BOMBS
CANT BEAT US
OUR ORANGES
CAME THROUGH
MUSSOS 'LAKE'

LEFT: Liverpool suffers a pre-Christmas raid on December 21, 1940.

BELOW LEFT: A row of taxis destroyed by bombing in London's Leicester Square.

BELOW RIGHT: The ruined city centre of Coventry still smoulders after the air raid on November 14, 1940.

BOTTOM: Firemen tackle a blaze at a factory in Birmingham after a raid in November 1940.

Bombing of Coventry

The Blitz was widened beyond London and the industrial city of Coventry was targeted on the night of November 14. The city's weak defences offered little opposition to the Luftwaffe, allowing them to utterly devastate the city centre, causing great loss of life. The German tactic was to drop incendiary devices to start fires that would continue to wreck the city long after the bombers' departure. A long list of other cities were bombarded but Britain's seaports and shipyards at Southampton, Liverpool, Bristol, Portsmouth, Plymouth and Glasgow were subjected to particularly severe raids. The raids petered out after the Germans invaded the Soviet Union in June 1941 and the Luftwaffe was redeployed east. By this time, tens of thousands of civilians had been killed and hundreds of thousands had been made homeless. Although Germany would continue to bomb Britain intermittently, the worst of the raids were over for British civilians. However, for the German civilians, the Blitz had barely begun.

DAILY MAIL   NOVEMBER 16, 1940
Homes for all in smitten city

Coventry, hard-smitten by as heavy a night of bombing as even London has suffered, has shown itself to-night as a city of good Samaritans. Throughout the suburbs and the city the well-to-do and the poor alike have thrown open their houses to the homeless. Hundreds of men, women, and children whose homes were wrecked 24 hours ago have been welcomed to-night in those of people they had never seen before.

In working-class districts particularly I saw hastily scrawled notices in the windows of house after house: 'Room for two,' 'Room for three,' 'Will take four children.' No one who knocked at these doors was refused admission. People who had lost everything were told by complete strangers, 'You're welcome to share everything we've got.'

The aftermath of death and suffering has been a wave of warm humanity. In schoolrooms, empty mansions, and church halls, the homeless have gone to sleep to-night. 'No one is without a bed, and no one has gone to sleep hungry,' a city council official told me. 'It's marvellous the way people have rallied round.'

As the people were preparing their makeshift accommodation gunfire was heard again to-night. But Coventry went on with the work of restoration. I saw men and women still living in the wrecks of their homes. On houses whose roofs had been blasted away the people had rigged makeshift covers. 'Hitler?' said one housewife to me. 'No fear! We stay put. And we're going to go on sleeping here.'

A pall of smoke hung over many areas of Coventry to-day. Two thousand high-explosive and thousands of incendiary bombs were rained indiscriminately on the city last night in a dusk-till-dawn air raid. Main streets were reduced to acres of rubble, and famous public buildings, cinemas, shops, houses, were obliterated. A thousand people were killed and injured and thousands more found themselves without homes. Yet the spirit of the people is unconquerable.

Only a shell of walls remains of Coventry's famous cathedral. Churches, public baths, clubs, cinemas, hotels, and hundreds of shops and business premises have been damaged. In the suburbs hundreds of houses have been demolished and thousands of people made homeless. The attack lasted eleven hours. It is estimated here that at least 100 'planes, arriving in waves, took part. The first raiders to arrive dropped incendiary bombs, and many fires were started. As the intensity of the attack grew, the din became terrific.

There are no greater heroes in the city now than the staff of a hospital which suffered a direct hit. The operating theatre was wrecked, but to-night doctors and nurses who have been working throughout last night and to-day are still on duty tending the wounded people being rescued from the debris.

MORE BOMBS ON PALACE
The King and Queen Escape Unharmed

GERMAN C.-IN-C. "IN THE FIELD"

THE King and Queen escaped injury yesterday when enemy 'planes deliberately bombed Buckingham Palace.

The King and Queen stay at home

Lowering British public morale was a key aim in the German High Command's bombing strategy and it proved to be a frightening experience for many, and affected everyone's life. Nevertheless, while every member of the population was touched in some way, they did not become demoralized. In fact, the constant attacks seemed to provoke the reverse effect to that intended – the sense of a nation pulling together; for bombs did not discriminate, no one, not even the King and Queen who remained in Buckingham Palace for the duration of the war, was spared the effects or the fear.

LEFT: A crater just outside the gates of Buckingham Palace was one of five, all caused by bombs dropped near to each other in September 1940.

ABOVE: Workmen labour to repair one of the areas of damage.

BELOW: Winston Churchill joined King George VI and Queen Elizabeth to inspect some damage in the grounds. The culprit was a time bomb dropped by a German raider.

TOP LEFT: **A policeman shows off some of the wreckage caused by the bomb that destroyed the Palace's North Lodge.**

ABOVE: **The North Lodge, next to Constitution Hill, received a direct hit in a raid in March 1941. A policeman died when one of the stone pillars fell on him.**

TOP RIGHT AND ABOVE RIGHT: **Following a night of heavy bombing, the Queen toured the East End, visiting the site of a bombed hospital and speaking to local families.**

DAILY MAIL   SEPTEMBER 12, 1940

Buckingham Palace hit by bomb

Buckingham Palace has now shared with Britain's humblest homes the fury of the Nazi raiders. Yesterday I walked round the gardens with Sir Alan Lascelles, the King's Assistant Private Secretary, and saw the effects of a time bomb which landed 6ft. from the Palace.

It exploded early on Tuesday - during another raid - wrecked part of the Princesses' swimming pool and smashed nearly every window in the north wing, including the windows of the royal suite.

The King and Queen spent the week-end at Windsor, but when the King returned to London yesterday he, the Queen, and Mr. Churchill, who lunched at the Palace, inspected the crater and also the damaged part of the Palace.

No one was hurt. Members of the household had been moved to another part of the Palace when the bomb was discovered near the Belgian Suite.

The windows of the King's and Queen's bedrooms and dressing-rooms; the Queen's bow-windowed sitting-room and the King's little balconied work-room were blown out. Showers of soot, glass and masonry poured into these rooms, covering the floors with thick dust and chipping walls and doors. The bomb - believed to be a 250-pounder - buried itself 10ft. deep, forcing up stone slabs on the terrace.

It demolished one wall of a Georgian-period building which was converted into a swimming pool about two years ago. This had previously been a conservatory.

The explosion broke in pieces some of the huge columns of the building. Masonry, weighing many tons, was flung into the air. Some of it was hurled over roofs and landed in the quadrangle. An underground shelter underneath the pool was also damaged.

Legacy of the bombing

Following the 'Fire of London' raid on the night of December 29, 1940, the capital suffered almost nightly bombing until May 1941. During the night of May 11 over 500 Luftwaffe planes dropped hundreds of high explosive bombs and tens of thousands of incendiary devices. Many important London landmarks were damaged that night, including the chamber of the House of Commons and Big Ben. This was the last great bombing raid on London, but one of the legacies of the months of sustained bombing, was the fear of the attackers returning.

LEFT: **The Lord Mayor of London spent New Year's Day 1941 inspecting the damage in Aldermanbury.**

BELOW: **The Guildhall suffered severe damage during the raid. Here, wreckage of the roof beams lies in the Banqueting Hall. It was to take years of careful restoration work post-war to return the building to its former glory.**

LEFT: The scene at St Bride's Street in London after a raid. The majority of the people were on their way to work and would need to salvage what they could from the premises and find alternative places to work.

BELOW LEFT: A quick and effective method for the police to give the 'All Clear'.

BELOW RIGHT: The Pioneer Corps was formed to help with clearance and salvage operations with the workers largely drawn from the unemployed. The Salvation Army was on hand to provide food and drink for them.

DAILY MAIL MAY 12, 1941

Biggest London raid

It had been a fantastic night. London was bathed in the golden glow of the full moon. Soon the mingled incendiaries and explosives turned parts of the city into an inferno. Rolling billows of smoke blotted out the moonlit sky.

Some commercial buildings were hit. But once more it was the houses of the people, rich and poor, that suffered most.

Over all was the roar of the guns, the whistle and crump of bombs, and the crackle of the fighters machine-guns high in the sky. Five hospitals were hit and there were casualties at three of them. One was a children's hospital.

At one hospital four wards were demolished, and twelve people, including a night sister and a woman dispenser, were killed. A sister saw the bomb tear its way through her ward and then explode in the one beneath. She at once started rescuing 18 men patients who were buried under the debris. With the help of nurses, she got them all out except one, who was killed.

Nearby, an earlier bomb had hit an A.R.P. rescue party depot. Two men were killed and six injured. Those who escaped had just finished extricating their colleagues when the hospital was hit. They immediately ran to the spot and helped nurses who were struggling with huge pieces of masonry beneath which some of the patients were trapped.

Women left the shelter in a block of flats to help the men fire-watchers and to salvage furniture when the roof of the flats was set on fire by incendiary bombs. They formed human chains to pass buckets of water for the stirrup pumps.

There was heavy loss of life when a bomb crashed through the roof of a London hotel and exploded in the basement, in which many of the 140 guests and employees were sheltering.

There were other casualties at a shelter, a rest centre, and a warden's post and a street market, where people were trapped. A cinema and several churches were struck. A club and an A.T.S. post also received direct hits.

BELOW: **Young women pick their way through the debris after the last major, and most devastating raid on London.**

RIGHT: **A postman tries to deliver letters in Watling Street, London.**

ABOVE LEFT: Men at work in the torpedo workroom.

LEFT: Inspection was carried out at all stages of production. Here the casings for naval shells are checked.

ABOVE: Shells arriving in the inspection shop at an ordnance factory.

BELOW: Inspecting shells at a Royal Ordnance factory. Quality control was very important in order to prevent the military being put at risk from its own equipment.

Munitions

Once the British government had established a military force, its next priority was to organize the production of the munitions with which that force could fight the war. Factory space, a labour force and raw materials were needed to produce weapons in large quantities. Some raw materials were imported but many were provided by 'salvaging' or recycling items already in the country. Teams of women and children, organized by the Women's Voluntary Service (WVS), toured from house to house, collecting metal in the form of tin baths, saucepans and old tin cans. Additionally, they collected scrap rubber, rags, waste paper and animal bones, all of which had some use in the production of weaponry.

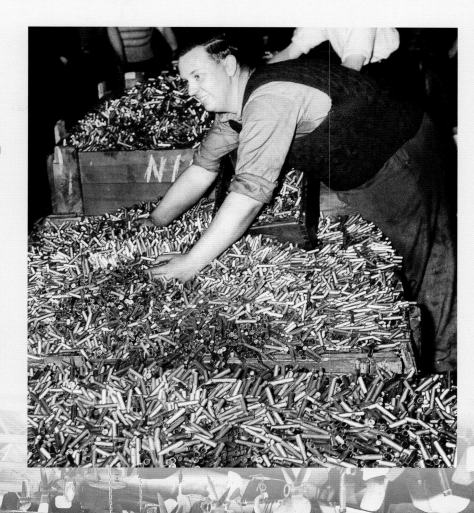

RIGHT: **Thousands of empty cartridge cases ready for filling.**

BELOW: **Every torpedo was 'tried out' and 'passed under working condition' before being dispatched to a Royal Navy ship.**

BELOW INSET: **A factory inspecting room which was 'working at emergency pressure, day and night, to produce small arms, spare parts and tools.' Britain had not spent money on armaments in the years after the First World War and consequently, when war broke out again, it was a race to provide the equipment the military needed.**

Lend-Lease

At sea, the Battle of the Atlantic was underway. It was vital that Britain could continue to be supplied by sea; the country's survival depended upon it. The essential convoys of supplies were under constant attack from both the Luftwaffe and U-boats, which were now able to operate from bases along the coastline of France, much extending their range. Most of the supplies came from the United States, but their cost was beginning to prove prohibitive to Britain's straitened wartime economy. President Roosevelt was willing to give any support (short of actual military involvement), despite the USA's reluctance to become involved in what it saw as an essentially European affair. Churchill appealed to him for help in March 1941, and Roosevelt persuaded Congress to pass the Lend-Lease Act. This allowed the United States to lend war materials to a country whose defence was seen as necessary for the ultimate safety of the States. The relationship between Britain and the United States was strengthened further when Churchill and Roosevelt met in August 1941. They issued the 'Atlantic Charter', in which they stated their mutual reasons for resisting aggression.

ABOVE: **President Roosevelt signs the Lend-Lease Act into law.**

BELOW: **A great merchant flotilla of British and Allied ships assembles near New York as they prepare to take war materiel to Britain under the Lend-Lease Act.**

LEFT: **An Allied merchant ship is guided through a minefield by means of semaphore.**

Italian defeats

Italian forces had invaded British Somaliland in August 1940. This had initially forced a retreat, but the British had begun to gather a large force of tanks in the area. This meant that when the Italian Army staged an invasion of Egypt from Libya in September, the British and Commonwealth forces were able to push them back to Benghazi with comparative speed. Abyssinia, which had been invaded and occupied by Italy in 1935, was also liberated. Mussolini faced a similar disaster in Greece; after invading in October 1940, the Italians met with stiff resistance and were pushed back to Albania by November 1940. To make matters worse, the British attacked the Italian Navy at Taranto, its main base, on November 11. Torpedoes were dropped by aircraft and were, for the first time, effective in shallow water – the British lost two planes, but the Italians lost half their fleet.

To reverse Italy's losses, Hitler intervened. His troops had been steadily moving across the Balkans, bringing Romania, Bulgaria and Yugoslavia under his domination. In April 1941 he ordered his Panzers southward to complete the invasion of Greece. He also strengthened the Axis Powers in North Africa. By the end of April his Afrika Korps, under the command of General Erwin Rommel, had driven the British out of Libya, back across Egypt and to within range of the Suez Canal.

BISMARCK SUNK
Scouter From U.S. "Spots" Her For The Navy

Sinking of the Bismarck

In May 1941 the German battleship *Bismarck* sailed from the Baltic to the Atlantic on a mission to attack the vital Atlantic convoys, where she could have done great damage. She was undoubtedly the greatest surface threat to their safety. As she passed through the Denmark Strait on May 24 she was intercepted by Britain's great battleship HMS *Hood*. The ships opened fire. The *Hood* received a series of direct hits and sank within minutes with the loss of 1415 men; only three survived. This served to further demonstrate the danger the *Bismarck* represented, and efforts to sink it were redoubled. Once the *Bismarck* was out in the Atlantic she was pursued by British warships and rather elderly torpedo-carrying Swordfish planes. Skirmishing by the Swordfishes disabled the *Bismarck's* steering mechanism leaving her vulnerable. The warships moved in and finished the ship off on May 27.

TOP LEFT: **German paratroopers board transport planes in Greece bound for Crete, to where the remainder of the Greek and British Armies had retreated.**

MIDDLE LEFT: **German paratroopers deploy in Crete with minimal equipment, as most of their supplies were dropped separately. This provided a twofold advantage to the Allies, for the Germans were outgunned, and much of their kit was captured.**

LOWER LEFT: **The Germans had taken control of Crete by the end of May 1941. Many of the Allied troops were evacuated, but about 18,000 were captured.**

BOTTOM LEFT: **South Africans charge through an Italian smokescreen in Libya.**

TOP RIGHT: **The Indian Army faces the Italians in Eritrea in April 1941.**

PANEL: **Survivors of the *Bismarck* are picked up by the Royal Navy.**

Soviets occupy Baltic States

Following the invasion of Poland and a German-Soviet treaty governing Lithuania, the Soviet Union forced the Baltic countries to allow the stationing of Soviet troops in their territories under pacts of 'mutual assistance'. Finland rejected the Soviet Union's territorial demands and was invaded by Communist forces in November 1939. The resulting conflict ended in March 1940 with Finnish concessions. France and the United Kingdom, treating the Soviet attack on Finland as tantamount to entering the war on the side of the Germans, responded to the Soviet invasion by supporting the USSR's expulsion from the League of Nations. In June 1940, the Soviet Armed Forces invaded and occupied the neutral Baltic States.

MOCK BATTLES AS HITLER MENACES

Finns Call Up More Men : Rumania Orders Ships Home

Va...

FINED £30,000 IN TWO DAYS

"EARNED CONTEMPT"

FINED £15,000 at the Mansion House yesterday for failing to register American stock, £29,107. Rol... merch...

at Ba... deli...

BEER SHORTAGE

ESSEX PUBLIC-HOUSES HAVE TO CLOSE

Public-houses in some parts of Essex are closing for one or two days a week owing to...

YOU CANNOT GIVE AWAY YOUR RATIONS

YOU cannot draw your meat rations...

"DADDY BRINGS MEAT IN HIS BOOTS"

CHILDREN TOLD TEACHER

"Daddy has been bringing home meat in his Wellington boots," children at an infants'...

ALLIES IN SUBURBS OF DAMASCUS

BRITISH and Allied troops were reported to-day to have smashed their way...

DAILY MAIL JULY 14, 1941

Stalin Toasts British Pact

Britain and Russia yesterday simultaneously announced the signing of a Pact declaring their full determination to defeat Hitler. The terms said:

1. The two Governments mutually undertake to render each other assistance and support of all kinds in the war against Hitlerite Germany;
2. They further undertake that, during this war, they will neither negotiate nor conclude an armistice or treaty except by mutual agreement.

The agreement came into force immediately on its signing in Moscow on Saturday by Sir Stafford Cripps, British Ambassador, and M. Molotov, Soviet Foreign Commissar. After the signing, Stalin joined in the toast to the Pact, drunk in champagne. Poland will be joined to the pact in the course of the next few days.

Negotiations between the Poles and the Russians have so far progressed speedily and satisfactorily. This is due as much to the willingness of the Poles to face the realities of the present situation as to the receptiveness of the Russians and their diplomatic contacts with the British and United States Governments. It would, of course, be paradoxical that the differences between these two neighbouring States, now allied to Britain for the overthrow of Hitler, should be allowed to remain unsettled.

Stalin's act in September 1939 when he occupied half Poland (by agreement with Hitler), will be repudiated. After this has been done, normal diplomatic relations will be restored and arrangements made for the release of the 200,000 Polish war prisoners held by the Russians, for service in the common cause.

THIS PAGE: **Russian tanks on patrol and in action on the battlefield in July 1941. Soviet armoured forces used a mix of self-propelled light anti-tank guns, which could move at great speed while firing rapidly, along with much larger tanks each equipped with a 6-inch gun set on a revolving turret.**

OPPOSITE TOP LEFT: **Russian Leader Joseph Stalin poses for an official photograph.**

OPPOSITE MIDDLE LEFT: **After the Finns recaptured territory from the Russians in the Petsamo region of northern Finland, the bodies of the Russian casualties were collected together ready for burial.**

The corpses were frozen in the positions in which they died.

OPPOSITE TOP RIGHT: **A German infantryman settles into a shell-hole to read the newspaper just received from home.**

OPPOSITE MIDDLE RIGHT: **At the end of July two Russian soldiers crouch**

behind their heavily-camouflaged machine-gun nest, poised for enemy approach.

OPPOSITE BOTTOM: **In January 1940 the frozen bodies of Russian soldiers lie along the roadside after the Battle of Suomussalmi in Finland.**

Germany invades Russia

On Sunday June 22, 1941, Hitler launched Operation Barbarossa, his invasion of Russia. He had reneged on the Nazi–Soviet Pact of 1939, and Stalin is thought to have been caught completely by surprise, despite the fact that the invasion force had been amassing for some time. Hitler had originally intended the attack for about a month earlier, but it had been delayed by a combination of weather and heavy fighting elsewhere. This would prove to be important as it gave the Germans less time to advance east and northwards before the winter began. Churchill immediately pledged support for Russia, and during the summer the Americans agreed to extend their policy of Lend-Lease to Russia.

Scorched-earth policy

At first the Russians retreated from the advancing Germans. They took anything that could be useful to the invaders with them and simply destroyed everything else – not just supplies but fields of ripening crops, bridges and railways: a complete scorched-earth policy. German troops were besieging Russia's second city of Leningrad by September, the Ukrainian city of Kiev fell in October and Hitler's troops had reached the outskirts of Moscow by the end of November. This was not as good for the Germans as it might have appeared. Not only was the bitter Russian winter now setting in, but the Russians were also well equipped to defend both Leningrad and Moscow. Towards the end of the year, on December 6, they launched a counter-attack against the Germans, who were now faced with the problem of surviving the savage weather as well as beating off the determined Russians.

LENINGRAD TOLD: "FIGHT TO THE LAST"

DRAMATIC CALL BY VOROSHILOV

TERRIFIC BATTLE RAGES FOR ODESSA

BIG R.A.F. FORCES GO OUT TO-DAY
TWO WAVES CROSS COAST

6,000 ARRESTS IN PARIS POLICE SWOOP TO-DAY

AUSTRALIA NAVY CHIEF:

OPPOSITE TOP RIGHT: **Women help to construct defences around Leningrad as the German forces advance.**

OPPOSITE MIDDLE RIGHT: **A woman and her two sons are among the last to leave their town. Following Stalin's orders, the inhabitants laid waste to it themselves.**

OPPOSITE BELOW RIGHT: **A residential district burns in Kiev, in the Ukraine.**

OPPOSITE LEFT: **Civilians are hanged by the Nazis near Smolensk. The Soviets intercepted this image of Nazi brutality and sent it to newspapers around the world.**

OPPOSITE BOTTOM: **The Soviets destroy anything that might be of use to the German armies as they retreat. It was the same tactic used by Russian troops to defeat Napoleon more than a century earlier.**

TOP: **German troops wait by the roadside while a burning village is searched.**

ABOVE: **German troops advance through a burning farm. The crops, farmhouse and farm vehicles were all destroyed.**

ABOVE RIGHT: **German troops pass the burned-out shell of the Electrical Industry building in Kharkov.**

BELOW: **The last inhabitants flee Kerch as German and Romanian divisions enter the city.**

DAILY MAIL   JUNE 23, 1941

Germans thrusting at Leningrad

German armies were last night reported to be making three main attacks in their great offensive against Russia along a front of 1,500 miles; from Finland towards Leningrad; from East Prussia towards Moscow; and from Rumania towards the Ukraine.

These distances are great. A hundred miles of difficult country lie between the Finnish frontier and Leningrad. Moscow is 600 miles from East Prussia. The Ukraine is almost immediately menaced, but the territory stretches 600 miles into Russia.

A fourth thrust is being made in Poland. Berlin radio claimed last night that German troops had crossed the Bug River, which flows in an arc around Warsaw. Long columns were said to have penetrated deep into Russian territory.

Berlin correspondents of Swiss newspapers said the Germans were using several thousand tanks to drive an opening in the Russian front and were expecting 'tremendous results.' The attack towards Leningrad is being made by German and Finnish divisions across the Karelian Isthmus - the battleground between the Soviet and Finland only 18 months ago.

Reports reaching Stockholm said a revolt which had broken out in Estonia was being successfully dealt with by Red troops. Some of the rebels seized ships in Tallinn harbour and opened fire on Russian troops in the capital.

Large formations of the Soviet Air Force have already attacked East Prussia, according to the Swiss radio. They were met by German fighters, and there were fierce and prolonged battles. German radio boasted of the superiority of the Luftwaffe over the Soviet air force. 'The German pilots,' said one of their war correspondents, 'found the Russian airmen completely inexperienced and they behaved like children.'

Three hundred divisions, or over 4,000,000 men will be locked in battle along this vast new front. Germany is estimated to have massed 125 divisions, including those she used against Greece - now policed by Mussolini. She has as allies 25 Rumanian and probably five or six Finnish divisions. Russia's western army is believed to consist of 150 divisions. Many others are available, but the state of their equipment is doubtful.

Pearl Harbor

On Sunday December 7, 1941, the war became a truly global one. Just before eight in the morning, Pearl Harbor, the US naval base in Hawaii, was attacked by almost 200 Japanese fighter planes. The strike came without a declaration of war and caught the navy completely unaware. An hour after the planes had returned to the six aircraft carriers which had escorted them, a second wave of a similar size struck. In total, 19 warships were damaged or destroyed and more than 2,400 people were killed. The scale of the destruction might have been even worse had the US Navy's aircraft carriers not been out on manoeuvres.

Tension between the United States and Japan had been mounting for some years. Japan desired to be the dominant power in East Asia, and the decline of Britain, France and the Netherlands had made this possible. However, the United States, with its presence in the Philippines and interests in the resources of the East Indies, continued to pose a major hurdle. Japan felt squeezed by the United States since Washington had imposed an oil embargo and aided China in the Sino-Japanese War in response to Japan's aggressive expansionism. Attempts to reach a diplomatic solution to their dispute failed as Roosevelt was anxious not to be seen as appeasing Japan in the manner that Hitler had been appeased before the war.

By November 1941, Japan's fuel supplies were running dangerously low and the navy resolved to capture the oilfields of the Dutch East Indies. Fearing that the United States might declare war as a result, and convinced that a war was one day inevitable, Japan launched a pre-emptive strike on the US fleet.

JAPAN INVADES MALAYA, THAILAND AND HONGKONG

Naval Battle in Pacific : Japanese Aircraft Carrier Reported

DAILY MAIL DECEMBER 8, 1941

Japan declares War on Britain and America

Japan to-night declared war on Britain and the United States after launching full-scale naval and air attacks on two of America's main bases in the Pacific - Pearl Harbour, in Hawaii, and Guam, between Hawaii and the Philippine Islands.

Already the Dutch East Indies have announced themselves at war with Japan, and the formal British and American declarations are expected in a matter of hours.

Quickly recovering from the first attacks, American warships steamed out of Pearl Harbour, and it was later reported that a Japanese aircraft-carrier had been sunk. Four Japanese submarines and six aircraft are also said to have been destroyed.

The Columbia Broadcasting System claims to have picked up a message saying that two British cruisers were sunk by Japanese planes attacking Singapore. This report is completely without confirmation. Another message, equally without support but well within the bounds of possibility, is

that Japanese warships have been engaged by British and American naval units in the Western Pacific. This report emanates from the Tokio correspondent of a Japanese newspaper in Shanghai quoting an announcement by Imperial Headquarters.

Early reports that Manila, the American base in the Philippine Islands, had been raided were followed by messages that all is quiet there, apart from aircraft taking off either on reconnaissance or to engage Japanese shipping.

Mr. Stimson, Secretary of War, has ordered the entire United States Army into uniform. This applies to 1,600,000, including thousands of officers and men who are on duty in administrative posts and hitherto have been allowed to wear civilian clothes.

To-night Mr. Roosevelt ordered the Army and Navy to carry out undisclosed orders, already prepared for 'the defence of the United States.'

OPPOSITE TOP RIGHT: Smoke and debris fill the air as the Japanese attack Pearl Harbor.

OPPOSITE MIDDLE RIGHT: The USS *Arizona* sinks, engulfed in smoke and flames.

OPPOSITE BELOW: Smoke billows from the USS *Shaw* turning the blue Hawaiian sky black.

TOP: The Japanese attack on Pearl Harbor disabled the US Pacific fleet allowing Japan to push into South East Asia with little opposition.

BELOW: The huge propeller and part of the hull of the *Arizona* protrude from the water after the attack.

ABOVE: Stunned Americans rushed to enlist in the armed services. Here men enrol for the US Army Air Force (USAAF) under the shadow of Lady Liberty in New York.

RIGHT: A line of Japanese battleships with the *Mitsu* nearest the camera.

'WE ARE IN IT, ALL THE WAY'—ROOSEVELT

'Setback at Hawaii: Our Pacific Bases Lost'

"GERMANY & ITALY AT WAR WITH US"

MEXICO TO SEND TROOPS THROUGH U.S.

CHINESE HELP FOR HONGKONG

America declares war

The day after Pearl Harbor, President Roosevelt delivered a speech to a joint session of Congress saying that December 7, 1941 was a 'date that will live in infamy' and requesting that Congress declare a state of war against Japan. Within hours both houses had voted overwhelmingly in favour of the war. Only one vote was cast against in either chamber, Congresswoman Jeanette Rankin from Montana opposed the war on account of her pacifist beliefs. Britain declared war against Japan on the same day. Three days later, on December 11, Japan's allies, Germany and Italy, declared war on the United States.

RIGHT: The President signs the declaration of war against Japan, just hours after delivering his speech to Congress.

BELOW RIGHT: Roosevelt is flanked by Vice President Henry Wallace, Speaker Samuel Rayburn, and his son, Captain James Roosevelt as he delivers his 'Infamy speech' in the House of Representatives.

LEFT: Factories engaged in war work were asked to put up this poster to inspire their employees.

BOTTOM: President Roosevelt addresses a joint session of the US Congress requesting a declaration of war against Japan.

TO ALL DEFENSE WORKERS . . .

The President of the United States said:

"I APPEAL . . .

"to the owners of plants
"to the managers
"to the workers
"to our own Government employees
"to put every ounce of effort into producing these munitions swiftly and without stint. And with this appeal I give you the pledge that all of us who are officers of your Government will devote ourselves to the same whole-hearted extent to the great task which lies ahead.

"We must be the great arsenal of democracy. For us this is an emergency as serious as war itself. We must apply ourselves to our task with the same resolution, the same sense of urgency, the same spirit of patriotism and sacrifice as we would show were we at war."

* * *

Let's get squarely behind our President's appeal.

* * *

Let's work together building that "GREAT ARSENAL OF DEMOCRACY" in record time.

*

Increase PRODUCTION! - That's our No. 1 job!

Let's go!

ABOVE LEFT: **Police in Paducah, Kentucky, exchange their patrol cars for pedal bikes in order to conserve rubber, an import from the East Indies, which would inevitably grow scarce.**

LEFT: **Americans register for sugar ration books, May 1942. Sugar was America's first rationed commodity of the war.**

BOTTOM LEFT: **The camp at Manzanar, California, that housed more than 60,000 Japanese citizens and Japanese Americans during the war.**

TOP RIGHT: **Japanese men leave a California hotel after being picked up by the FBI.**

BELOW: **Hundreds of residents of Tillamook, Oregon, meet to discuss civil defence in the event of a Japanese invasion of the West Coast.**

DAILY MAIL DECEMBER 9, 1941

Congress declares war on Japan

Marines with fixed bayonets guarded the Capitol to-day as the United States Congress formally declared war on Japan. They voted 25 minutes after President Roosevelt, in a message denouncing Japan's aggression, had called for this action.

Mr. Roosevelt was frequently and loudly cheered during his address. He described yesterday as 'a date that will live in infamy.' The United States, he said, was at peace with Japan, and at her solicitation was still in consultation with her Government's representatives. 'Indeed, one hour after Japanese air squadrons had commenced bombing the American island of Hawaii, the Japanese Ambassador and his colleague delivered to our Secretary of State a formal reply to a recent American message. It contained no threat or hint of war,' he said.

'It will be recorded that the distance of Hawaii from Japan makes it obvious that the attack was deliberately planned many days or even weeks ago. During the intervening time the Japanese Government has deliberately set out to deceive the United States by false statements and expressions of hope for continued peace.

'The attack yesterday on the Hawaiian Islands has caused severe damage to American naval and military forces. I regret to tell you that very many American lives have been lost. In addition, American ships have been reported torpedoed on the high seas between San Francisco and Honolulu. Yesterday the Japanese Government also launched an attack against Malaya.

'Last night, Japanese forces attacked Hongkong. Last night Japanese forces attacked Guam. Last night Japanese forces attacked the Philippine Islands. Last night the Japanese attacked Wake Island. And this morning the Japanese attacked Midway Island.

'As Commander-in-Chief of the Army and Navy, I have directed that all measures be taken for our defence, but always will our whole nation remember the character of the onslaught against us. No matter how long it may take us to overcome this premeditated invasion, the American people in their righteous might will win through to absolute victory.'

American women at war

Women took on many paid jobs in temporary new munitions factories and in old factories that had been converted from civilian products like car manufacturing. This was the 'Rosie the Riveter' phenomenon. 'Rosie the Riveter' became a cultural icon representing the American women who worked in factories that produced munitions and war supplies.

Women also filled many traditionally female roles that were created by the war boom – as waitresses, for example. And they worked in jobs that previously had been held by men – such as bank teller or shoe salesperson. Nearly one million women worked as so called 'government girls,' taking jobs in the federal government, mainly in Washington DC, that had previously been held by men or were newly created to deal with the war effort.

Women began to gain more respect and men realized that women could work outside the home. They fought for equal pay and made a huge impact on the United States workforce.

ABOVE: **With New York skyscrapers looming through the clouds of gas, US army nurses at Fort Jay, Governors Island, New York, wear gas masks as they drill as part of defence precautions in December 1941.**

ABOVE RIGHT: **Mrs Morton Stern is taking the fingerprint of Mrs Mabel Glenby at the headquarters of the American Women's Voluntary Service in New York City. In the background are other women who are registering**

for war work. The American Women's Voluntary Service (AWVS) announced that 10,000 women had enrolled for defence training courses in the first week of the war.

RIGHT: **Women workers, trained for aviation work, are busy on the assembly line of the Glenn L Martin aircraft plant in Baltimore in February 1942, where hundreds of bombers are being turned out. They have taken the place of the men called up for the armed forces.**

BELOW: **Members of the American Women's Voluntary Service being received by the US squadron commanders, Lowell Beatty of New York and Harold Baker of Westchester Unit in December 1941. The women reported for instruction in coast guard patrol duty at 97th Street and Hudson River.**

US Tanks for the Front Line

Design of the M-3 Tank commenced in July 1940, and the first were fielded in late 1941. The US Army needed a good tank immediately, not a perfect tank later and this, coupled with Great Britain's demand for medium tanks immediately, meant the M-3 was brought into production by late 1940. It was well-armed and -armoured for the period, but was withdrawn from front line duty as soon as the M-4 Sherman became available in large numbers.

TOP RIGHT: The last step in the manufacture of the M-3 medium tank was to lift them by crane into flat cars, clamp them down and cover them with tarpaulin. Cars loaded with US tanks, having been thoroughly tested by army officers, would leave Detroit's Chrysler Tank Arsenal on a daily basis.

MIDDLE RIGHT: At the start of the war, the Watervliet Arsenal was the only gun manufacturing plant in the US to turn out the famous 16 inch and 14 inch cannons for the army and navy. This

view of the shop where the big guns were made, show them in position in the huge machines where the workmen will turn them into finished products after 12 months of hard work. Under its defence programme the government increased its personnel at the arsenal and kept the machines running 24 hours a day.

BOTTOM RIGHT: This photograph, taken at the Chrysler Tank Arsenal in April 1942, shows a medium tank being carried overhead for convenience and quick handling. Fewer rivets

were used in the new medium tanks than in the M-3s; but for those that remained in the blueprints, 125-ton 'cold' riveting machines such as this would save much time and leave no doubt that the rivets were in to stay.

BELOW: Soon after war was declared the grim reality of the conflict comes to San Francisco as big ramparts of sand bags are hastily constructed in front of one of the telephone company's buildings.

JAP TANKS POUR INTO BURMA

South East Asia falls to Japan

The conflict in the Pacific escalated rapidly. On December 10, the British Navy suffered an appalling blow when two of its largest battleships, the *Repulse* and the *Prince of Wales*, were sunk by Japanese bombers. Japan made several lightning-fast strikes throughout the area, and by the end of the year the US bases at Guam and Wake Island had been captured. Hong Kong fell on Christmas Day, 1941. Japanese forces moved swiftly in an attempt to seize control of South East Asia following the attack on Pearl Harbor and their run of victories in Malaya, Hong Kong, Thailand and the Philippines. They now launched attacks throughout the Pacific; in January 1942, Manila, the Dutch East Indies, Kuala Lumpur and Burma were invaded.

Burma

This put the Allies under immense pressure. British troops in Malaya were forced to retreat to Singapore by February. The city fell on February 15, and about 80,000 British and Australians were captured. Later in February, Japan attacked Australia itself, bombing the northern city of Darwin. Then the Japanese landed on the island of Java on February 26, defeating British and Dutch naval forces in the Battle of the Java Sea. By early spring, it seemed that the Japanese were almost invincible. British troops had been forced to withdraw across the mainland of Burma towards the Indian border, and the Japanese were continuing to capture islands throughout the western Pacific.

DAILY MAIL   DECEMBER 27, 1941
Hong Kong's last stand

The full story of the Battle of Hongkong was issued by the War Office last night.

It starts with December 8, when the Japanese attacked our troops on the mainland and we withdrew into 'Gindrinkers Line,' and ends with Christmas Day when the last of the island garrison was forced to capitulate.

The Hongkong garrison consisted of two British, two Canadian, and two Indian battalions and the Hongkong Volunteer Defence Force. These were: the 2nd Bn. Royal Scots, 1st Bn. Middlesex Regt., a battalion of Winnipeg Grenadiers, a battalion of Royal Rifles of Canada, 2/14th Bn. Punjabis, and 5/7th Bri. Rajputs, with the normal complement of R.A., R.E., R. Sigs. units, and auxiliary services. Units of the Royal Navy and the Hongkong Naval Volunteer Reserve and detachments of Royal Marines co-operated with the military forces.

The geographical features of the colony, states the War Office, its isolation, and the fact that its only aerodrome was on the mainland precluded the possibility of air support.

On the morning of December 8, a Japanese division, with a second division in immediate reserve, crossed the frontier on the mainland. Demolitions were made, and our troops withdrew. There was patrol activity, and a men-carrier patrol ambushed and annihilated a Japanese platoon on Castle Peak road.

On the morning of December 11, strong enemy pressure developed on our left flank, held by the Royal Scots. Two companies were driven off by heavy mortar fire, but the situation was stabilised by using all available reserves. The Royal Scots suffered severe casualties. By midday it was decided to evacuate all the mainland except the Devil's Peak position.

Stonecutters Island was heavily bombarded all day. The island was evacuated during the night of the 11th after demolitions had been made.

The island was sporadically bombarded by artillery and from the air. The civil population was reported to be calm, but their morale considerably shaken. Monetary problems and rice distribution gave cause for serious anxiety.

December 13 was a difficult day.

The enemy sent a delegation to negotiate surrender. The proposal was summarily rejected by the Governor (Sir Mark Young).

On December 16 serial bombing and artillery shelling were increased. One enemy aircraft was brought down into the sea.

On the 17th aerial bombardment was directed against the Peak wireless station and other places. No military damage resulted.

On December 22 the enemy landed further troops on the north-east coast. A counter-attack on the 21st from Stanley towards Ty Tan Tak had failed, although a certain number of the enemy were killed at the cost of about 100 Canadian casualties.

On December 23 some ground on Mount Cameron lost during the night was recaptured by the Royal Marines, but counter-attacks by the force at Stanley towards Stanley Mound failed. However, the Middlesex Regiment successfully repulsed a determined attack at Leighton Hill.

It was impossible to conceal the fact that the situation had become exceedingly grave. The troops, who had been fighting unceasingly for many days, were tired out. The water and food supply was desperate. The reservoirs and depots were in enemy hands.

On December 24 the enemy continued to subject the garrison to heavy fire from dive-bombers and mortars, and by means of incendiary bombs set the countryside all round Mount Cameron on fire.

On December 25 the military and naval commanders informed the Governor that no further effective resistance could be made.

America's first victories in the Pacific

The Battle of the Coral Sea took place from May 4-7, 1942. American aircraft carriers off New Guinea intercepted a Japanese invasion force heading towards Papua and the southern Solomon Islands. This was the first naval battle in which all the fighting was done by the pilots of planes launched from aircraft carriers; it was also the first defeat for the Japanese. There were losses on both sides, but the Japanese fleet was turned back with the loss of an aircraft carrier, making the Coral Sea America's first victory in the war with Japan.

Midway and Guadalcanal

One month later, four more Japanese aircraft carriers were destroyed at the Battle of Midway, severely reducing their capabilities. This heralded a clear change in the Allies' fortunes; they were beginning to gain the advantage in the Pacific in terms of the balance of both air and sea power. Allied attacks were launched in the Solomon Islands, and the first landings took place at Guadalcanal on August 7. At first there was little resistance, but the Japanese troops were very swiftly reinforced and fierce fighting was to rage for the rest of 1942. Naval battles also continued, and the Americans inflicted further heavy damage to the Japanese Navy and to a supply convoy off Guadalcanal in November. The island was finally won in February 1943 at a cost of thousands of lives. Within days the Americans moved to assist the Australians in pushing the Japanese out of New Guinea. The Australians had already dealt the Japanese their first defeat of the war at Milne Bay in September 1942, and the addition of the Americans was sufficient to win back control of the island by the end of 1943.

OPPOSITE ABOVE: A Japanese soldier skirmishes with British troops in Burma.

OPPOSITE MIDDLE: A scout group of British, American, Chinese and native Kachin troops wade through a river in the Burmese jungle.

OPPOSITE BELOW: One of the US Navy's amphibious trucks brings supplies ashore at New Caledonia in the South Pacific. American troops landed on the Free French island-colony in April 1942.

TOP LEFT: A US bomber attacks a Japanese plane in New Guinea.

MIDDLE LEFT: American soldiers man a howitzer launch during an attack in Burma.

MIDDLE RIGHT: Men of Britain's 14th Army patrol through swamps in Burma.

ABOVE LEFT: Marines board an LCM landing craft in the Aleutian Islands before setting off to push the Japanese off Kiska Island.

LEFT: US troops fire on Japanese positions on the Aleutian island of Attu. The Japanese navy attacked the Aleutians to try to divert the Americans from Midway.

The Americans arrive in Britain

Meeting in Washington in December 1941, Churchill and Roosevelt agreed that the Allies should concentrate on winning the war in Europe before turning their attentions fully towards the Pacific theatre. This 'Germany First' policy had its critics, but it was agreed that the US and Britain would be stronger fighting together, and that logistically Britain had to confront the Nazi threat first. Nevertheless, the US would keep piling the pressure on Japan and won some key battles at Coral Sea and Midway during 1942.

American troops had begun landing in Britain within weeks of the attack on Pearl Harbor and Hitler's subsequent declaration of war on the US; throughout 1942 they were to arrive in vast numbers. These were the GIs (their equipment was stamped 'General Issue'; hence the name) and they were largely welcomed in Britain.

The GIs proved especially popular with children – they were widely seen as purveyors of treats that had become impossible to find, such as chocolate and sweets. They were also very popular with some British women, some 20,000 of whom would become 'GI brides' by the end of the war. As a result of this, many British men would complain that the Americans were 'oversexed, overpaid and over here'.

RIGHT: **Just seven weeks after the raid on Pearl Harbor and America's entry into the war, US troops began landing in Britain.**

TOP RIGHT: **An American soldier enjoys a Bank Holiday fair in Hampstead.**

MIDDLE RIGHT: **American marines land in Iceland on their way to Britain.**

ABOVE: **A US Jeep makes for an unusual sight amongst the London traffic.**

ABOVE: **General Eisenhower watches Charlton Athletic take on Chelsea in the Southern Cup Final at Wembley Stadium.**

RIGHT: **Britain was awash with Allied troops. Here Winston Churchill visits Czechoslovak troops with the Czechoslovak President Edvard Benes.**

RIGHT BELOW: **American tank crews on manoeuvres in England.**

FAR RIGHT ABOVE: **Eleanor Roosevelt tours buildings destroyed in the London Blitz, October 1942.**

FAR RIGHT MIDDLE: **Many women were thrilled that the arrival of the GIs meant that luxury items such as stockings became easier to obtain. Until then many women had painted their legs to give the impression of a seam.**

BELOW: **British and American troops arrive in port in advance of the Allied invasion of North Africa, November 1942.**

Stalingrad

Russia's Red Army had managed to hold out over the winter of 1941 and even had some success in pushing the Germans back from Moscow in January. By late spring, however, the German Army had regrouped and a new campaign was planned. This time the intention was to strike towards the Crimea in the south, which would ultimately enable the Germans to take control of the Caucasus where there were significant oil reserves.

In June and July the Germans captured Rostov and Sevastopol, but this initial success was not to last. The German Army turned north in August, heading for the important city of Stalingrad, where their advance was slowed by Russian resistance. It finally ground to a halt in the suburbs of Stalingrad itself, and the Germans had to settle in for a long siege instead of a swift advance. Stalingrad was desperately defended, with every patch of ground contested bitterly, and then the Russians launched a counter-offensive as the winter of 1942 began. They inflicted heavy casualties on their enemies and eventually surrounded the Germans to both the north and south of the city. Trapped between the relieving troops and the city's desperate defenders, the German Sixth Army and the Fourth Panzer Division awaited help from a relieving army, as well as urgent supplies of all kinds.

ABOVE: **Russian marines engage the Germans on the Black Sea coast, July 1942.**

TOP RIGHT: **New Red Navy torpedo boats set out on a mission in the Black Sea.**

MIDDLE RIGHT: **A family crouch over the body of their father, murdered during a massacre in the town of Kerch. The bandaged man on the left of the picture was wounded in the head during the massacre and lay still, covered with earth and corpses until the Germans departed.**

RIGHT: **The scene of Nazi terror against the civilian population of Russia in Rostov-on-Don.**

BELOW: **The ruins of Stalingrad's factory district, where much of the fighting took place.**

Russian victory

It was astonishingly cold – the temperature reached 24 degrees below freezing – and the Germans lacked winter uniforms, food and medicine. Ammunition was also running low, but Hitler refused to allow their surrender – nor could he manage to supply them, effectively condemning the Army to a form of mass suicide. By December there was no longer much doubt about the ultimate result, and January 31 saw a massive defeat for the Germans south-west of Stalingrad. On February 2, 1943 the German commander, Paulus, finally surrendered, disobeying Hitler. The Russians took over 90,000 prisoners, amongst whom were 24 generals; many more, on both sides, had died. This was the German Army's greatest-ever defeat and a major turning point on the Eastern Front. The Russians now began to push the Germans back to the west.

ABOVE: **Stalingrad residents welcome reinforcements from the Red Army.**

TOP RIGHT: **Soldiers raise the Red Flag above a building in a recaptured part of Stalingrad.**

RIGHT: **Once the Germans had been defeated, these women were free to emerge from the basement which had been their home for the duration of the battle.**

BELOW: **Many Soviet civilians were trapped in the city and had to make their homes among the rubble, in basements, or even in shell holes.**

DAILY MAIL FEBRUARY 1, 1943
Stalingrad army wiped out

Field-Marshal Paulus, Commander-in-Chief of the German Sixth Army and Fourth Tank Army at Stalingrad, was captured by the Russians yesterday a few hours after he had been promoted to the highest rank by special proclamation from Hitler's headquarters.

He was seized with his staff when Soviet troops stormed the Ogpu headquarters in the heart of the city and completed the greatest disaster that has befallen Germany in this war.

It is now revealed as a disaster of unsuspected propor-

tions. Instead of 220,000 men, the trapped army consisted of 330,000 troops, it was announced by Moscow in a special communique last night.

In addition to the Sixth Army, the Fourth Panzer Army has been trapped and destroyed. Thirteen German and two Rumanian generals and 46,000 troops have been captured. Five thousand were taken prisoner with Marshal Paulus yesterday. Booty taken between January 10 and 30 includes 744 aircraft, 1,517 tanks, and 6,523 guns.

Resistance and collaboration

During the Second World War the Nazis controlled a vast swath of Europe from France to the Soviet Union. Throughout their occupied territories and vassal states the Germans found people prepared to work with them and those intent upon working against them. Those who collaborated usually did so because they were sympathetic to Nazi ideology or were pragmatists willing to work with whoever was in charge. They assisted the Germans by forming puppet governments, deporting Jews and arresting members of the resistance; some even joined voluntary units of the dreaded Waffen SS. Those opposed to German occupation or to Nazi ideology joined organized resistance movements or engaged in individual acts of defiance. Their activities ranged from hiding Jews and sabotaging communications to killing collaborators and providing intelligence to the Allies. Many others did not actively participate in resistance or collaboration and simply tried to survive the occupation – these people have sometimes been criticized as passive collaborators.

The reaction to the German occupation was not uniform across Europe; there was inevitably more resistance activity wherever the German presence was stronger and German rule more direct. Different national groups also responded to the German presence in different ways and some nations even welcomed the Germans as liberators from other oppressors – such was the case in Croatia and Estonia where the Germans were regarded as liberators from Serb and Russian domination respectively.

ABOVE LEFT: **Marshal Pétain inspects French troops at Châteauroux, in unoccupied France.** Pétain ruled Vichy France in collaboration with the Nazis in order to spare southern France from direct German rule. The Vichy government actively supported Nazi racial policies against the Jews, and thousands were rounded up, sent to concentration camps, and later transported to death camps in the east.

TOP RIGHT: **Quisling gives the Nazi salute as he inspects German troops in Norway.**

TOP LEFT: **Vidkun Quisling awaits his trial** in Oslo at the end of the war. The name of the wartime Premier of Norway, who was appointed upon the orders of Hitler, has become synonymous with collaboration.

ABOVE RIGHT: **The Allies drop supplies to the Resistance in Nazi-occupied Belgium.**

ABOVE MIDDLE: **'Here lives a collaborator'.** Anyone suspected by the Resistance of collaborating with the Germans might have woken to find this sign posted on their front door during the night.

BELOW: **French Resistance fighters are drilled on the edge of a field close to the treeline** so they can take cover.

Uprisings in Warsaw

From November 1939 Warsaw's Jewish population was forced to move into a ghetto, which was sealed off from the rest of the city the following year. Jews from all over Poland and Europe were sent to live in the Warsaw Ghetto where thousands died from starvation and disease. From July 1942 the Nazis began a major purge of the Ghetto and hundreds of thousands of people were sent to their deaths at Treblinka. In early 1943, after news of the exterminations had reached the Ghetto, the remaining population rose up in rebellion. Using weapons that had been smuggled in or improvised, the rebels held out against the German Army for almost a month. Thousands were killed during the uprising and the survivors were deported to death camps or executed on the spot.

The following year the Polish Home Army, the main Polish resistance movement, rose up in rebellion hoping to liberate Warsaw before the fast-approaching Soviet troops arrived. The uprising began on August 1, 1944 and the 50,000 strong Polish Home Army met with some early successes. However, the Germans soon sent in reinforcements and the Luftwaffe began a relentless bombardment of the city. The rebels were slowly worn down and no relief came from Soviet forces, which had stopped just short of the city – ostensibly on the orders of Stalin who did not want the Polish Home Army to take over. With more than 200,000 dead and much of the city destroyed, the rebels surrendered on October 2, 1944. The Russians seized the city three months later.

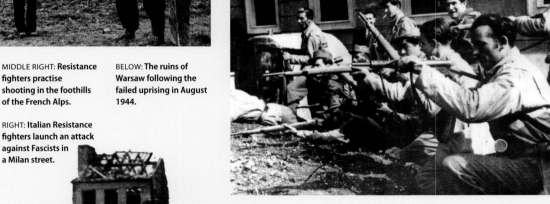

ABOVE: **This still from a film smuggled out of France reveals daily life in the French Resistance. When possible, the day began with the raising of the Tricolor.**

TOP RIGHT: **In hunger and despair, members of the Polish Resistance await the arrival of the Nazis following their surrender.**

MIDDLE RIGHT: **Resistance fighters practise shooting in the foothills of the French Alps.**

RIGHT: **Italian Resistance fighters launch an attack against Fascists in a Milan street.**

BELOW: **The ruins of Warsaw following the failed uprising in August 1944.**

El Alamein

The start of 1942 saw something of a stand-off in North Africa; both sides were regrouping on either side of the Gazala Line. German commander, Field Marshal Rommel, launched his next attack on the British in May, as the Germans were attacking in Russia. His Army outflanked the British and forced them to make a rapid withdrawal to Tobruk – which was lost by June. Following that, the British Eighth Army retreated eastwards to El Alamein. Here it was possible for them to be reinforced, both swiftly and to a considerable extent, from the Suez Canal. There were sustained German attacks during July and August, but the British were able to hold the defensive Alamein Line. They were ready to strike back by October, under the inspirational command of General Montgomery, who was sent to lead the Eighth Army in August. During the night of October 23, 1942, an enormous artillery bombardment began, followed by a frontal assault against Rommel's forces. Progress was steady though slow initially, but the advance picked up speed and Rommel began to retreat on November 3. The Germans were then quickly pushed back into Libya.

ABOVE: **Part of the vast Allied armada heading to the North African coast during Operation Torch.**

MIDDLE RIGHT: **Troops bring stores ashore on the North African coast during the Torch landings.**

BELOW RIGHT: Wading through the Mediterranean Sea, American troops come ashore in Algeria.

BELOW: **Headed by a standard bearer, US troops march towards an airfield near Algiers on the first day of Operation Torch.**

TOP RIGHT: **An American-built Maryland bomber of the South African Air Force strikes a German supply convoy in the Libyan desert.**

Operation Torch

Five days later, on November 8, a large-scale invasion of French North Africa was launched under the command of US General Dwight Eisenhower. It was known as Operation Torch, and had the honour of being the largest seaborne expedition in history until it was dwarfed by the Normandy landings.

Stalin had been demanding that the Allies open a second front in Europe to relieve some of the pressure on the Red Army, which was defending an enormous front. Roosevelt agreed with the strategy in principle, but was advised against it by his generals. Churchill was also sceptical; he had authorized 'a reconnaissance in force to test the enemy defences' at the French port of Dieppe in August 1942. It was a disaster. The force was withdrawn after only nine hours, by which time thousands of troops – mostly Canadians – had been either killed or captured. Instead, Churchill advocated opening a new front in North Africa. By capturing Tunisia, the Allies would severely disrupt the enemy's supply lines and could engage them on two fronts.

TOP: **Medium bombers of the US Army Air Force in the Middle East are seen flying in formation over the desert in late October 1942. The planes are camouflaged so that they blend into the background colour. Their role was to harrass the supply lines and bases of the Axis forces in North Africa.**

ABOVE: **American troops wade ashore at Arzeu,**

Algeria, having been delivered from their ships by landing craft.

RIGHT: **General Eisenhower and General Giraud inspect a Guard of Honour of French troops during a victory parade in Tunis, Tunisia, in May 1943.**

BELOW: **The Torch landings, commanded by General Eisenhower, began on November 8 with troops**

deployed at Safi and Casablanca in Morocco, and on beaches at Algiers and Oran in Algeria. After brief conflicts with French forces, Admiral Darlan, commander of Vichy France, ordered a ceasefire on November 11, and thereafter French cooperation was assured. The Allies now began to close in on the Axis armies from both sides, forcing them into Tunisia.

ROMMEL FORCED BACK 15 MILES

ALLIES SMASH HIM IN 3-DAY BATTLE

1,000 ITALIANS TRAPPED IN A PASS

Reuter's correspondent on the Tunisian front cabled this afternoon:

An Italian battalion of

ORPHAN GIRLS TRAPPED IN FIRE: 36 DIE

Eighty-five girls were trapped when fire swept an orphanage attached to St. Joseph's Abbey of Poor Clares in Cavan, Eire, early to-day.

It was officially announced this afternoon that the death roll is 30 and that 30 bodies have been recovered. The orphans include Miss Maggie Smith, the parents the

3 RUSSIAN COLUMNS ARE DRIVING FOR KIEFF

THREE Soviet columns, after a spectacular 100-

THE HOME GUARD ABSENTEE SAID—

"MY WIFE WON'T LET ME GO TO PARADES"

A man of 27 accused at Old-street court to-day of fail to attend for Home have the only is that The Pr

BLACK

CLOSING

EVERY THR HAR

A.P. c front cab The Ger which re Thala yesterday and Ame With

Arms and Prisoners

Pushing Germany out of Africa

There was little resistance to the Allied landings, and Admiral Darlan, the commander of Vichy France, whose forces were occupying the area, ordered a ceasefire just two days later. He also appealed to the French Navy to leave Toulon, where they were based, and join the Allies. Hitler immediately scrapped Marshal Pétain's collaborationist Vichy government and ordered the full occupation of France, which took place on November 11. The French immediately scuttled their fleet to deny the Germans additional naval power.

By the end of January 1943 Montgomery's Army had pushed the Germans back westward from Egypt through Libya and General Eisenhower was pushing east. Trapped between the two, the position of the Axis forces was hopeless. Rommel himself left for Europe, handing over to General von Arnim. The Axis army – about 250,000 men – surrendered to the Allies in May.

RIGHT: **Old Glory, the American flag, flies above the ruins of a North African town.**

BELOW: **The liberated French population of Algiers give the V-for-Victory sign as American troops march through the town.**

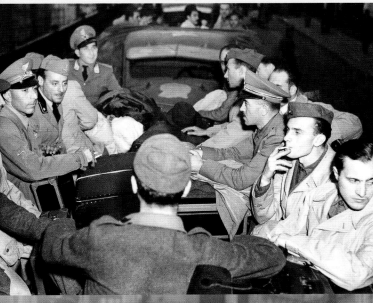

ABOVE RIGHT: **The first operational task of the United States Army in the European theatre of operations, the occupation of French North Africa, was begun on November 8 by US Rangers simultaneously landing at strategic points. Here, an American officer is in conversation with villagers at a point near Oran where a landing was made without opposition.**

ABOVE LEFT: **America's General Eisenhower (centre) with Britain's General Montgomery (right). After pushing the Germans out of Africa, the two men would lead the Allies to victory in western Europe.**

LEFT: **Italian soldiers are driven through the streets of Algiers on their way to internment camps. American troops were charged with maintaining order as locals poured onto the streets to jeer at the POWs.**

BELOW: **Captured Italians are driven through Algiers to internment camps shortly after the Torch landings.**

The home front in Britain

In Britain women had begun to be conscripted into war work or the forces in December 1941. By 1943, 90 per cent of single women were either serving in the forces or working in war industries – such as munitions and armaments factories and shipyards – replacing the men who were now in the armed forces. They also worked in agriculture, where there were eventually some 80,000 'land girls' in the Women's Land Army.

Life in Britain during the war was often difficult as bombing raids continued and most things were in short supply. Everything from clothes to food and from soap to petrol was rationed and people were encouraged to 'make do and mend', by repairing and reusing everyday items.

With everybody devoting their lives to fighting for their country in some way, there was widespread agreement that post-war British society would have to change to benefit the majority of the population. The way forward was set out in the Beveridge Report, which became an unlikely bestseller. In it, Sir William Beveridge proposed that a system of social security for everyone should be set up after the war, with a National Health Service and a system of family allowances.

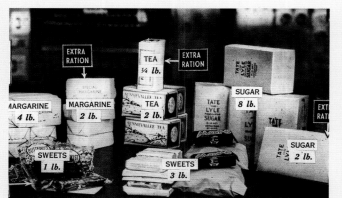

ABOVE: **Land girls reap the harvest on a Buckinghamshire farm.**

LEFT: **German attacks on merchant shipping would bring Britain dangerously close to running out of essential supplies. Bacon, butter and sugar were the first products to be rationed, quickly followed by other foodstuffs and household goods.**

BELOW LEFT: **A member of the Women's Land Army ploughing reclaimed land on a farm in Bedfordshire.**

BELOW: **German bombing resulted in temporary evacuations and diversions, further disrupting daily life in Britain.**

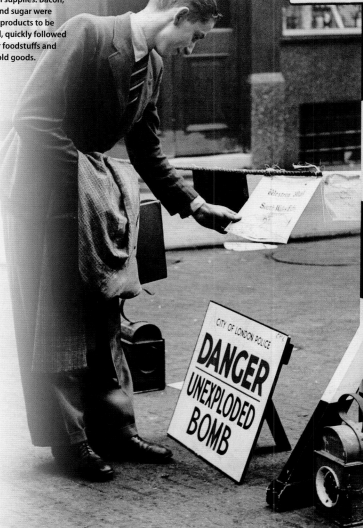

Easing of restrictions

By 1943, the Allies had superiority in the air, but smaller-scale bombing raids did still occur, particularly over London, and usually in response to attacks on German cities. Perhaps the most tragic incident happened on the night of March 3 during a minor raid in the East End of London; it was not directly attributable to the enemy, however. People were hurrying to enter Bethnal Green Underground station to take shelter, when somebody lost their footing at the top of the stairs and fell. Pressure from behind meant that those in front could not stop, and the resulting crush caused the deaths of 178 people.

The end of the Blitz had brought some small relaxation in regulations, though rationing continued. Early in 1943 it was ruled that lights in railway carriages could be left on when trains were standing at stations (they had previously been extinguished so that the trains – and thus stations – could not be easily detected from the air), and it was later agreed that traffic lights could be used; pedestrians were allowed to carry undimmed torches.

TOP LEFT: **Making a phone call between protective sandbags in London.**

LEFT: **British people were encouraged to 'Dig for Victory' by growing vegetables wherever there was space. Even bombsites were converted into allotments.**

TOP RIGHT: **Schoolboys take tea in the garden of their damaged home following a raid.**

MIDDLE RIGHT: **Clothes rationing began in Britain on June 1, 1941. Owing to a shortage of material, people were encouraged to 'make do and mend' by repairing old garments.**

BOTTOM RIGHT: **Despite being bombed out of their office building, work continues in the street.**

The Baedeker Raids: Britain blitzed again

The Baedeker Raids took place from April 1942 to the end of June. The name came from Baedeker travel guides of Britain, as the press reported that this was how the targets were selected. Instead of attacking the industrial towns and cities, suddenly all the picturesque tourist cities such as Bath, Norwich, Exeter, Canterbury and York became targets. They did not have the air defences of the larger cities and consequently 1,637 people were killed with 1,760 injured. Over 50,000 homes were lost. It was believed that these raids were in response to the Allied bombing of the medieval centre of Lübeck in northern Germany. It had been targeted as a base used to supply German troops on the Russian front.

ABOVE: **The ruins of St Andrew's Church in Bath, gutted by fire after a Baedeker raid in April 1942.**

RIGHT: **York's 15th-century Guildhall in flames after a raid in retribution for RAF attacks on Baltic ports.**

BELOW: **Searching for victims in the ruins of St John's Roman Catholic Church in Bath which received a direct hit. One of the priests was killed.**

ABOVE LEFT: **A comic moment as Pioneer Corps come across a relic from the past in the rubble of bombed Bath.**

ABOVE: **During a raid on the city of Cambridge in August 1942, the University Union Society's building suffered the effects of blast damage.**

LEFT: **Bomb damage to one of Bath's beautiful Georgian Crescents.**

BELOW: **Thick grey dust covered the houses and roadway after the havoc caused in a Bath thoroughfare by the bombers.**

Working conditions

Even though women in Britain daily proved their abilities as part of the workforce, they were paid considerably less than their male counterparts. The average woman's pay in 1943 was £3 2s 11d, just over 50 per cent of the £6 1s 4d that was the average male pay. Additionally, working conditions were often very basic. As munitions factories had generally been converted from peacetime production – not necessarily of munitions – or were hastily converted or constructed buildings, and as many of the machine tools were used for jobs for which they were not initially intended, safety was frequently a serious concern. Many factories were designed for men and far fewer workers than employed during the war, so that facilities like toilets and rest rooms were in short supply. Normal working hours were long and when there were calls for increased production, such as after the retreat from Dunkirk, the working day could be extended, so that women found themselves working from 8 am to 7 pm.

TOP LEFT: Women in the 'Pick and Shovel Brigade'. At a new aerodrome somewhere in East Anglia about 100 women and girls undertake navvies' work with zest and enjoyment. Here, they are laying pipes for drainage on each side of the runway.

MIDDLE LEFT: These women, filling sandbags, were the first to be employed to clear air-raid debris and help make buildings safe.

LEFT: Mrs E Glassett, drilling wing spars for a Halifax bomber, had been a sales assistant in a womenswear shop in London's West End. Like many women she gave up her peacetime job to go into the factories.

ABOVE: Miss Louisa Lines, aged 20, formerly a Yorkshire cotton machinist, painting along the scuppers of a nearly finished merchant ship. Women were fast taking their places with men in the shipyards – painting, plate marking, and generally carrying out tasks which before the war were considered hard even for men.

TOP LEFT: **Mrs Flannigan, a woman bricklayer, works to repair bomb damage to a Southern Railway arch in London.**

ABOVE RIGHT: **A woman works on making a shell casing at a factory in southern England.**

ABOVE: **In January 1941, Britain's first dustwomen assumed their roles in Ilford. The council employed 'eight comely dustbin-emptiers'.**

RIGHT: **'She-navvies' cheerfully wheel barrow loads of heavy stones at a railway goods yard.**

Bombing Germany

For the first two years of the war, Britain did not launch a comprehensive air offensive against German cities. There was strategic bombing of military and industrial targets within Germany, but it was not until 1942 that Britain began raiding the country with the intention of breaking civilian morale. Arthur 'Bomber' Harris took charge of Bomber Command in February 1942 and began planning for the aerial bombing of German cities. The test case for the new tactic was the historic city of Lubeck in northern Germany, which was struck on the night of March 28, 1942. The town's old buildings were easily set alight by the incendiary bombs dropped by the RAF, causing widespread destruction and loss of life.

1,000-bomber raids

Two months after Lubeck, Harris assembled his bombers for a strike against Cologne, an industrial city on the Rhine. Operation Millennium, as it was codenamed, employed 1,047 aircraft, making it the largest fleet yet seen in aerial warfare. The raid was originally intended for Hamburg, Germany's second-largest city and a major site of U-boat production, but it was switched to Cologne because of poor weather. On the night of May 30, the aircraft flew in a tight stream, maintaining height and speed, both to avoid collisions and to limit German radar detection. Although some of the crews missed their intended target, almost 900 planes bombed Cologne, releasing 1,455 tons of bombs, two-thirds of which were incendiary devices.

ABOVE RIGHT: **Members of the German Safety Service tackle a blaze caused by incendiary bombs.**

RIGHT: **An American Liberator bomber plunges towards the ground after being damaged by anti-aircraft fire.**

LEFT: **Low-flying RAF bombers strike a power station in Cologne.**

BELOW: **Berliners clear away debris following an air raid.**

Hamburg and Dresden

The RAF proceeded to relentlessly bomb Germany by night, and from 1943, they were joined by the American Air Force (USAAF) which bombed by day. This round the clock bombardment never directly achieved its aim of forcing Germany into submission by breaking civilian morale, but it did play a vital role in wearing Germany down in preparation for the overland invasion.

In late July 1943, the RAF and the USAAF launched Operation Gomorrah, a series of devastating raids on Hamburg. Almost 3,000 sorties were flown over the city leading to the deaths of an estimated 40,000 people, most of whom perished in a great firestorm that engulfed the city on the night of July 27. A firestorm caused by a heavy raid on Dresden killed tens of thousands of people in February 1945. Dresden was singled out for the raid because it was an important transport hub and was being used to send troops and supplies to the Eastern Front. The death toll was higher than might have been expected because Dresden's population had swelled in number as a result of the thousands of refugees who had poured into the city in the empty trains returning from the front.

TOP: **The Mohne Dam is successfully breached by a bouncing bomb during the 'Dambuster' raids of May 1943.**

ABOVE LEFT: **A B17 Flying Fortress crew study their new remote-controlled chin-turret which provided better protection against frontal fighter assaults.**

ABOVE RIGHT: **Despite massive damage to the tail of this B17, the pilot managed to return from his bombing mission over Germany and land safely back in Britain.**

FAR LEFT: **US airmen report back to an officer following a successful raid on industrial sites near Berlin. The markings on the back of this navigator's jacket indicate the number of missions he has completed.**

LEFT: **Factories and an airfield in Berlin burn after heavy bombing. Initially, Berlin was spared the worst of the aerial onslaught because it was too far away for the RAF to mount a sustained campaign. However, improved technology and the arrival of the** Americans changed that and Berlin was bombed severely from November 1943 until the last months of the war.

ABOVE: **A Swastika is draped over a bombed-out building to mark Hitler's 55th birthday in April 1944. Despite the relentless bombing campaign, there was no revolution against the Nazi regime. Some continued to support Hitler, others feared his terror network or Soviet reprisals; the rest became stoically resigned to their fate.**

ENEMY FLEET
DODGES BATTLE

WAR MAY END "IN THE SPRING"
REPORTED STATEMENT BY CANADA'S PREMIER

1,000th LETTER
TO HIS WIFE IN CANADA
HIS 1,000th letter to his wife in Montreal has

HITLER SENDS
3 MORE DIVISIONS
TO THE BALKANS

Allied offensives in the Pacific, 1943–44

Midway proved to be the last great naval battle for two years. The United States used the ensuing period to exploit its vast industrial potential to produce ships, planes, and trained aircrew. At the same time, Japan, lacking an adequate industrial base or technological strategy, a good aircrew training programme, or adequate naval resources and commerce defence, fell further and further behind. In strategic terms the Allies began a long movement across the Pacific, seizing one island base after another. Not every Japanese stronghold had to be captured; some, such as Truk, Rabaul, and Formosa, were neutralized by air attack and bypassed. The goal was to get close to Japan itself, then launch massive strategic air attacks, improve the submarine blockade, and finally (only if necessary) execute an invasion.

In November 1943 US Marines sustained high casualties when they overwhelmed the 4,500-strong garrison at Tarawa. This helped the Allies to improve the techniques of amphibious landings, learning from their mistakes and implementing changes such as thorough pre-emptive bombings and bombardment, more careful planning regarding tides and landing craft schedules, and better overall coordination.

The US Navy did not seek out the Japanese fleet for a decisive battle, as Mahanian doctrine would suggest (and as Japan hoped); the Allied advance could only be stopped by a Japanese naval attack, which oil shortages (induced by submarine attack) made impossible.

ABOVE: 'Wildcat' fighter planes lined up and ready for US Navy and Marine pilots at an airfield on Guadalcanal Island in 1943. Although US Marines had withdrawn from the Island, the Marine Air Force was still there fighting hard with Army and Navy pilots.

Burma 1943

The Japanese invasion of Burma in 1942 had successfully cut off supply routes to China along the Burma Road and placed Japanese troops dangerously close to the Indian border. Japanese commanders had hoped that Indian forces in the area would revolt against the British. However, although some captured soldiers were formed into an army to fight against the Allies, colonial Indian divisions, which had fought alongside British troops in North Africa, were redeployed to Burma in 1943 where they fought with great distinction. Now under the overall command of Lord Mountbatten, British troops were reinforced and received greater air support, enabling them to maintain defensive positions deep in the Burmese jungles; the employment of guerrilla tactics would result in some successful campaigns against the Japanese. Major General Orde Wingate formed and led the 77th Indian Infantry Brigade, otherwise known as the Chindits, which adopted the tactic of 'Long Range Penetration', operating in columns deep inside enemy territory, sabotaging infrastructure and ambushing Japanese troops. Although they were eventually ordered to withdraw as air-drops became more difficult, the Chindits had proven that damage could be inflicted on the Japanese in difficult jungle territory.

BELOW: **Somewhere in the Burmese jungle, General Frank Merrill and some of his staff discuss new methods to hamper the Japanese campaign.**

OPPOSITE ABOVE LEFT: **American soldiers wave a greeting from one of the convoy ships arriving at an Australian port, with thousands of US troops and war materiel in June 1942.**

ABOVE: **Native stretcher bearers in New Guinea rest themselves and their casualties in the shade of a coconut grove en route from the front lines near Buna to hospitals in the rear. In skirmishes and large engagements, United States troops killed over a thousand Japanese in five days.**

The liberation of Italy

The Allied victory in North Africa in May 1943 altered the state of play in the Mediterranean, making an attack on Italy possible. Italy was in bad shape: the country had lost an estimated 200,000 soldiers in North Africa; more than 200,000 were fighting on the Eastern Front; and about 500,000 were deployed in the Balkans. So when American, British and Canadian troops invaded Sicily in July 1943, the island fell within just six weeks. This rapid defeat in Sicily, combined with the devastating bombing of the mainland, led to the overthrow of Mussolini by the Fascist Grand Council; he was arrested and sent to prison.

In September, the Allies had crossed to the mainland and the new Italian government surrendered. However, this did not bring peace as the German troops in the country continued to resist the Allied advance. Italy was now treated as another of Germany's vassals: Jews were rounded up and deported to Auschwitz, partisans were executed and the country was plundered of its historic artworks. German glider pilots even rescued Mussolini from his remote mountain prison and made him leader of their new puppet state, the 'Italian Social Republic'.

TOP FAR LEFT: **The people of Naples greet the Allies after having seen off the Germans themselves.**

TOP LEFT: **Roman women give a rapturous welcome to Allied troops.**

TOP RIGHT: **Italian soldiers in Sicily surrender.**

UPPER MIDDLE RIGHT: **Anzio lies in ruins in the aftermath of Allied raids in preparation for the landings in January 1944.**

LOWER MIDDLE RIGHT: **First news of Italy's surrender reaches London. However, the fighting would get much worse once the Germans took over.**

ABOVE: **As food grows scarce, the grounds of Milan Cathedral are turned into agricultural land.**

LEFT: **A church in Turin damaged during Allied air raids on the major industrial centres in northern Italy on August 8, 1943.**

The fall of Rome

After encountering some initial difficulties at Salerno, the Allies raced through southern Italy in September 1943. They reached Naples at the end of the month to discover the population of the city had already rebelled and pushed the Germans out. The lightning advance ground to a halt in November after the Germans retreated to the 'Gustav Line', a highly defendable position running across the country from the Tyrrhenian to the Adriatic Seas.

Attempts to break the Line during the winter proved costly to the Allies, so a surprise landing was made north of the Gustav Line, at Anzio, on January 22, 1944. In February the Germans counter-attacked in this area and the Allied advance came to a halt. To relieve the pressure on their men at Anzio, the Allies launched an invasion across the Gustav Line at Monte Cassino, the site of an ancient Benedictine Abbey. The town did not fall for three months, on May 18 – and then only after it and the Abbey had been completely reduced to rubble with great loss of life. With the Gustav Line breached, the Allies linked up with their comrades at Anzio and marched on Rome, liberating the city on June 4, 1944.

Mussolini executed

German forces continued to resist in Italy for almost a year, and it was not until April 29, 1945 that they finally surrendered. The day before, Mussolini and his mistress had been captured and executed by Italian partisans. Their bodies, along with fifteen others, were hung upside-down from the girders of a petrol station in Milan.

TOP RIGHT: **Monghidoro, just south of Bologna, is liberated by the Allies in October 1944.**

MIDDLE RIGHT: **British troops kick down the door of SS Headquarters in Florence.**

BELOW RIGHT: **Italian partisans search for German stragglers in the town of Cesena following its liberation.**

BOTTOM: **Seventeen merchant ships in the liberated Italian port of Bari are bombed in a surprise German raid in December 1943.**

DAILY MAIL FEBRUARY 16, 1944

Cassino Abbey bombed to a ruin

Front-Line troops of the Fifth Army watched in awed silence to-day the destruction by bomb and shell of Cassino Abbey. They looked on at the terrible bombardment with memories of comrades who had fallen under the guns of the Germans entrenched behind the abbey walls.

It had to be done - this razing of one of the great monuments of the Western World. And it has been done thoroughly after repeated warnings and with all due consideration for civilian life.

Seven waves of Fortresses, Mitchells, and Marauders have reduced the monastery to ruins. When I turned away from the scene an hour ago, the great, grey oblong monastery was nothing but a jagged silhouette against the pale blue sky. The German guns mounted in the abbey have been silenced. No longer is it the strong fortress dominating Cassino and denying us access along 'Highway Six' to Rome.

Doubtless there will be argument for many years to come about the deed that was done between 9 a.m. and 2 p.m., but I don't believe there was one man on our side of the Rapido Valley to-day who felt any regret or remorse, or, indeed, any other emotion save acute interest.

The attack was directed not only against the monastery but against the system of pillboxes and strong-points on the slopes below it.

TOP LEFT: **American artillery pounds Monte Cassino in February 1944. The abbey was initially spared, but the Allies began shelling it to deny the Germans a key** observation post on the Gustav Line.

ABOVE LEFT: **The Abbey lies in ruins after the battle.**

ABOVE: **Not a building is left undamaged during the Allied offensive on Monte Cassino.**

JAP FLEET SMASHED—Nimitz

14 Major Units Sunk or Damaged: 350 Jap Planes Destroyed

1944: Japan in retreat

The hard-won success of Guadalcanal led to a determined advance, codename Operation Cartwheel, by Allied forces through the Solomon Islands and New Guinea during 1943. Japanese forces had a major HQ in the town of Rabaul on the island of New Britain, garrisoned by around 100,000 troops; this now became a strategic goal for the Allies in the Pacific Campaign. In the Battle of Tarawa, a heavily fortified atoll that held the key to the recapture of the Marianas, the Allied beach landings in November were met by the first heavy Japanese resistance at the beachhead to date; this would provide useful experience for future Allied landings such as Iwo Jima – but with a high cost in casualties. In the game of chess played out in the Pacific Islands, the steady pushing of the Allied forces could only have one conclusion but the delaying tactics of the totally committed Japanese Imperial Army made progress slow and the loss of life very high – on both sides. But the first months of 1944 proved the tide had turned against Japan.

ABOVE: Marines on the littered beach at Tarawa covered their ammunition and other gear with camouflaged shelter-halfs in case the Japanese tried an air attack.

ABOVE RIGHT: A sub-machine gun in one hand and a grenade in the other, a soldier marches at the head of his men in pursuit of Japanese defenders of New Britain Island in the South-west Pacific. US troops, in a two-pronged drive, advanced to new positions on the north and south coasts of New Britain and by March 27, 1944, were less than 170 miles away from the major Japanese base at Rabaul.

RIGHT: US Marines attack a Japanese stronghold during the landing at Tarawa, where some of the 'bloodiest fighting of the campaign took place', to establish an Allied bridgehead on this central Pacific base. Two Marines – barely visible in their camouflaged cloaks – can be seen crouching behind the shattered stumps of palm trees, having tossed dynamite sticks, seen exploding on the Japanese stronghold.

BELOW: Marines advance across desolate Darry Island in the wake of fleeing Japanese, as they took Eniwetok Atoll in the Marshall Islands. The palm trees were either uprooted or defoliated by the bombardment before the leathernecks came ashore to clean out the holed-up Japanese in February 1944.

TOP LEFT: US Marines plunge through the surf at Cape Gloucester, New Britain, after disembarking from a landing craft to push a jeep to shore. An amphibious vehicle nears the beach during landing preparations on the south-west Pacific island on December 26. Some Marines carry stretchers so that the wounded can be removed promptly to medical stations. US landing forces captured the twin air strips on Cape Gloucester in the initial attacks and then pressed on inland in their campaign against the Japanese.

TOP RIGHT: American Marines wade ashore at Cape Gloucester, New Britain.

ABOVE RIGHT: A Japanese soldier, cornered by US Marines on Namur Island, holds out his arms in surrender while another Japanese digs his way out of a blasted blockhouse where twenty Japanese were trapped. Namur was the northern part of Kwajalein Atoll and one of the Japanese island fortresses in the Central Pacific taken by US forces leading up to the seizure of Kwajalein in the Marshall Islands, February 1944.

MIDDLE LEFT: American assault troops splash across a shallow stream, near Aitape, where they formed small patrol groups to seek out Japanese defenders of the coastal base on Northern Guinea. US amphibious forces stormed ashore at Aitape and at two points flanking Hollandia to the west on April 22, 1944, gaining control of

an additional 150-mile stretch of the northern New Guinea coast for the Allies. Supplementary landings six days later aided in blocking escape routes for an estimated 60,000 Japanese troops entrapped in that area of the south-west Pacific island.

LEFT: US amphibious tanks line a beach, bringing in supplies to American Marines who landed on Japanese-held Emirau Island in the St Matthias group of the south-west Pacific. In the background, an amphibious car pulls a truck ashore, while troops form a chain in the surf to convey materials to the beach. US Marines captured the island on March 20, 1944, to complete encirclement of Japanese remnant garrisons on New Britain, New Ireland and the Northern Solomon Islands.

D-Day

Preparations for the invasion of Occupied France had proceeded apace in Britain throughout the winter of 1943 and the spring of 1944. The Dieppe raid in 1942 had cost many lives, but it had also shown that it was going to be virtually impossible to capture and hold a major French port. 'Operation Overlord' was therefore planned to land on the less well-defended Normandy beaches to the east of the Cherbourg peninsula. This meant that a vast invading army would have to be both deployed and supplied without the advantages of a proper harbour, so artificial 'Mulberry' harbours were built to be towed across the English Channel to the landing beaches. In preparation for the invasion, special landing craft and amphibious vehicles were built, and large numbers of troops started to assemble in southern Britain. In addition, a pipeline named 'PLUTO' was laid across the seabed from the Isle of Wight to Normandy to ensure this enormous army had sufficient supplies of oil once the invasion was underway.

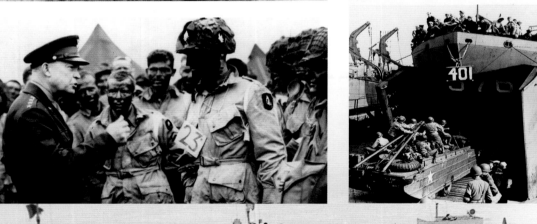

TOP RIGHT: **American soldiers train for the Normandy landings. Barrage balloons were floated across the Channel to offer some protection against enemy aircraft.**

ABOVE RIGHT: **General Eisenhower, Supreme Commander of the Allied invasion, plans 'Operation Overlord' from his headquarters in Britain.**

TOP LEFT: **The American army trains for D-Day at Slapton Sands in Devon. The beach was selected for its similarity to Utah beach.**

MIDDLE FAR LEFT: **General Eisenhower addresses camouflaged paratroopers just before they fly off on their mission to drop behind enemy lines in Normandy in the early hours of D-Day.**

MIDDLE LEFT: **A 'duck' is loaded onto its transport. These vehicles were ideal for seaborne invasions as they functioned both on land and water.**

BOTTOM: **The last items of equipment are loaded onto the transports ahead of D-Day.**

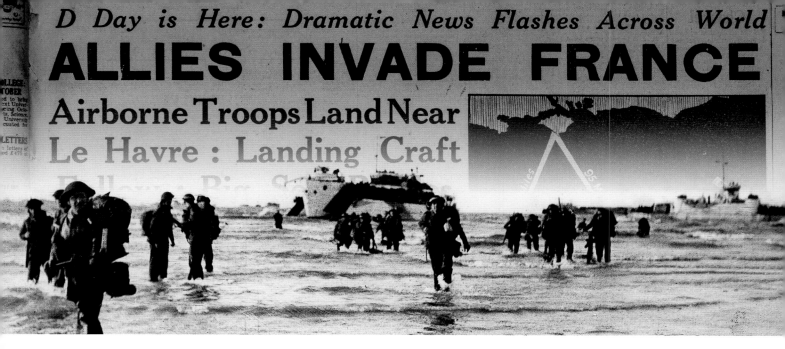

D Day is Here: Dramatic News Flashes Across World

ALLIES INVADE FRANCE

Airborne Troops Land Near
Le Havre : Landing Craft

The landings

The overall commander, General Eisenhower, gave the order for the long-awaited attack on the Normandy beaches to begin on June 6, 1944: D-Day. Soon after midnight a vast invasion fleet of nearly 7,000 vessels closed in on the designated beaches, and parachutists and glider-borne troops landed behind German lines in Normandy. At first light, after an initial assault from thousands of aircraft, the invasion proper began.

Five beaches were designated for the landings; the Americans came ashore at the westernmost beaches, codenamed 'Utah' and 'Omaha', while the British, supported by the Free French, landed further east at 'Gold' and 'Sword' beaches. The landing at 'Juno', in the middle of the two British beaches, was undertaken by the Canadian military, under the command of the British.

By the end of the first day some 130,000 men had landed in Occupied France and were able to establish a bridgehead in Normandy. This had come at a cost of many lives, especially at Omaha beach, where the preliminary aerial bombardment had missed the German defences along the sea wall. As the Americans came ashore, the Germans fired relentlessly from their pillboxes, gunning down hundreds of men before the beach was finally taken.

UPPER MIDDLE LEFT: **An aerial view of Omaha beach on the morning of D-Day. Military vehicles attempt to exit the beach while small dots of men and beach obstacles can be seen in the water.**

UPPER AND LOWER MIDDLE RIGHT: **American troops come ashore in Normandy.**

LOWER MIDDLE LEFT: **American soldiers await their fate in a 'Higgins Boat' as it approaches Omaha Beach.**

TOP: **Red Cross personnel and British infantry wade onto the beaches on 'D-Day+1', June 7, 1944.**

LEFT: **The Allied armada sets sail for Normandy in the early morning light of June 6, 1944.**

WE ADVANCE 20 MILES INLAND—Officia

Germans Admit Big Retreat in Carentan Area : St. Lo Ablaze

CAUMONT IS REACHED

A retreat of several miles in the Carentan area and breeches in their line towards St. Lo were admitted by Berlin to-day. Supreme Allied H.Q. said that we definitely hold Carentan, thus discounting reports that the Germans were back in the town.

Our patrols south of Bayeux have pushed 20 miles inland, and Supreme H.Q. revealed that Caumont had been reached.

Cherbourg Blockaded

Perfect Fighting Weather in The Channel

IT'S perfect fighting weather in the Channel to-day.

The wind is light and in the south-west—meaning an off-shore wind on the Normandy coast, where the water will be smooth in the lee of the land.

A breeze is raising no more than tiny ripples on the calm sea.

Visibility is perfect, with the Straits of Dover drenched in sunshine and the skies cloudless.

It is still coolish with the thermometer at about 55 degrees—and

U.S. TO FRANCO: STOP AID TO NAZIS

SWEDES AGREE TO CUT BALL-BEARING SUPPLIES

IT was learned in Washington to-day that Mr. Carlton Hayes, U.S. Ambassador in Madrid, has been instructed to ask Spain to ban all vital war materials to Germany such as olive oil, hides and wool.

It was announced to-day that an agreement with the Swedish S.K.F. ballbearing firm has been completed, which will result in a very substantial reduction in the exports of ball bearings to Germany. No details were disclosed.

Meanwhile, a strong demand for a complete economic blockade of Germany has aroused criticism of British ... an point to ...

WOUNDED AR
HOME IN HOURS

AIR AMBULANCES RUS THEM TO SURGEONS

"Evening News" Reporte

GREAT new possibilities in evacuation of wounded fr the battlefields of Europe opened up by the use of air a bulances.

The first of these made the t to France from an airfield Southern England yesterday.

When airfields are establishe Normandy it will mean wounded will be able to rece first-class medical treatment this country within a few hour the injury, with a conseq saving in life and suffering.

I saw men carried from Douglas Dakotas on stretc who were wounded during recent push by the bigg convoy yet to leave America ...

DAILY MAIL, JUNE 7, 1944

The last act

June 6, 1944, will stand as one of the memorable days of all time. Upon this day was launched the greatest act of war in history - the invasion of Europe. This day saw well begun the campaign which will end the war in an Allied victory.

The Germans are beaten, and they begin to know it. Rome was one portentous symbol in their darkening sky. The Allies have the advantage in men, material, morale - everything. On the Eastern Front Russia awaits her moment. No secret weapon or tactical trick can save the Third Reich now.

This is the thought that must be uppermost in our minds as we watch unfolding the gigantic combined operation of the Allied land, sea, and air forces.

'The battle,' says Mr. Churchill, 'will grow constantly in scope and intensity for many weeks to come.' It will go well at one moment and not so well at the next. The fortunes of war will not always favour us.

After nearly five years of mingled triumph and disaster the British people are not likely to be led astray by excessive hope or unreasoning despair. Rather will they respond to the words of the King, who last night asked for a revival of the crusading spirit which sustained us in the dark days.

A great team

There have been warnings from high places. 'A long period of greater effort and fierce fighting lies ahead,' says President Roosevelt. General Eisenhower gives an inspiring Order of the Day to his troops, but, he says: 'Your task will not be an easy one.'

These warnings spring not from apprehension but from a just appraisal of the situation. They are based on the confidence so well expressed by General Montgomery: 'We are a great allied team.'

The mighty forces sweeping across the Channel are equipped with all the best that modern science and ingenuity can provide, and are trained to the last ounce. Supporting them is the terrifying punch of 11,000 war-planes, and transporting them are 4,000 large vessels, besides many thousands of smaller ones, backed by the power of six battleships and numerous other naval craft.

We can but marvel at the extent and intricacy of the operation. Beside these hosts of craft and myriad of aeroplanes, the record armadas of North Africa and Sicily become small.

According to plan

Of the actual fighting we know little, but things are going well. 'The operation is proceeding in a thoroughly satisfactory manner,' says Mr. Churchill, and nothing could be more emphatic. It may be that these landings are among the feints which the Prime Minister mentioned some weeks ago. The Germans appear to expect landings elsewhere. Let them speculate. We are content to wait on events.

Events are inspiring enough. The largest massed airborne landing yet attempted anywhere has been successfully made. Other troops have pushed several miles inland from the beaches.

There will be many conflicting reports in the next few days. Those which do not come from official sources or accredited correspondents should be treated with reserve.

The first three days will be the most critical. If our fine men, who carry with them all our thoughts and hopes, can establish themselves firmly during that time, the first big obstacle will have been victoriously overcome.

LEFT: A snapshot of Omaha beach after the initial landings hints at the vast scale of Operation Overlord. During D-Day, over 130,000 men were brought ashore in nearly 7,000 vessels.

TOP LEFT: German prisoners carry an injured comrade as they load onto boats destined for detention camps in Britain.

TOP RIGHT: After facing down German guns, Allied soldiers had to contend with other parts of Germany's coastal defences. Mines and barbed wire were two such impediments.

MIDDLE: Troops start to move inland after securing a beachhead.

ABOVE: Wooden slat and wire runners are offloaded. They were vital for getting the thousands of vehicles off the beaches.

Liberation of France

The Germans were not prepared for the invasion force to come ashore at Normandy. They had been fooled by considerable decoy activity into believing that the attack would come along the coast near Calais. Nevertheless the fighting was bitter and the men encountered stiff resistance across Normandy. Within a few days the Allies began linking up their five beachheads as ever more troops poured ashore. All the plans for increasing and supplying the invasion force worked and, on June 27, American forces captured the port of Cherbourg. On July 8 Caen was taken after fierce fighting and the Allies began to push out of Normandy towards Paris.

A second invasion force landed in the south of France near Toulon on August 15 and drove the Germans northwards along the Rhone valley. In all their advances the Allies were given invaluable assistance by the French Resistance, who harried the retreating Germans. The village of Oradour-sur-Glane in central France was to pay the price for increased resistance activity: members of the 2nd SS Reich Panzer division massacred the entire village on June 10 as they made their way to the front in Normandy.

Liberating troops finally reached Paris on August 24, where serious street fighting had erupted some days earlier. French troops under the command of General Leclerc were given the honour of being the first to enter the city. They were followed a day later by the leader of the Free French, General Charles de Gaulle, who was treated to a rapturous welcome, despite the residual threat of snipers.

TOP FAR RIGHT: **Refugees hurry past an upturned German military vehicle and its dead driver in a Brittany village.**

MIDDLE FAR RIGHT: **A French civilian takes her frustrations out on a German prisoner as he is marched through the streets of St-Mihiel at gunpoint.**

FAR RIGHT: **French villagers watch as German prisoners are marched through the village of Ouistreham at 'Sword' Beach on the Normandy Coast.**

ABOVE RIGHT: **Eight days after D-Day, the leader of the Free French, General Charles de Gaulle, lands on the Normandy beaches.**

RIGHT: **A German soldier surrenders to the Allies days after the invasion.**

BELOW: **German POWs are marched through Cherbourg by American troops.**

"PARIS IS LIBERATED"—KOENIG

50,000 Maquis Win 4-day Battle in City : Police Seize the Prefecture : Hundreds of Thousands of Civilians Give Aid

GREAT ALLIED SWEEP

FORWARD TO THE SEINE

LORD MAYOR TO PARIS: 'WE SALUTE YOU'

THE LAST TIME HE SAW PARIS

ON OTHER PAGES TO-DAY

DAILY MAIL   AUGUST 26, 1944

Germans in Paris surrender

THE battle for Paris is over. General Leclerc's tank columns broke into the capital early yesterday and in less than 12 hours' fighting smashed German resistance. The end came suddenly last evening when Leclerc, according to the Patriot radio, delivered an ultimatum to the general commanding the German garrison. The two, with the Maquis chief of Paris, then went to Montparnasse Station, where the terms of the capitulation were signed.

Under these, the German general at once ordered the cease fire. His men, unarmed, were to assemble at selected points to await orders. Their arms were to be piled and handed over intact.

At about the time Leclerc dictated his terms to the German, and while fighting was still in progress, General de Gaulle entered the city. Huge crowds greeted him with the 'Marseillaise' and cries of 'Vive de Gaulle!' to which he replied: 'I wish simply and from the bottom of my heart to say to you, Vive Paris!'

Later, in a broadcast to the people of Paris, General de Gaulle declared: 'France will take her place among the great nations which will organise the peace. We will not rest until we march, as we must, into enemy territory as conquerors.' De Gaulle said that France has the 'right to insist' that she shall never again be invaded by Germany.

TOP: De Gaulle makes his way through the crowds on the Champs Elysees in Paris.

ABOVE: French armoured divisions pass through the Arc de Triomphe in Paris.

RIGHT: German troops surrender to the Americans at Metz.

BELOW: The spire of Rouen Cathedral towers above a city in ruins.

The liberation of the Low Countries

From France, the Allies raced into Belgium and liberated Antwerp and Brussels in the first week of September 1944. From Belgium, the Allies could have concentrated their forces on the industrial Ruhr region of Germany, but General Montgomery feared that an attack on the well-defended Siegfried Line would be too costly. Instead, he devised 'Operation Market Garden,' a plan to outflank the Siegfried Line through the Netherlands. His audacious operation involved dropping troops behind enemy lines to capture vital crossing points over a series of Dutch rivers and then following through with a swift ground invasion. The early stages were successful, but the British 1st Airborne Division met with strong German resistance at Arnhem on the Lower Rhine. The overland troops sent to relieve them were held up and then withdrawn, having sustained heavy casualties. Operation Market Garden was called off and the northern Netherlands remained under German control until the last months of the war. The Germans finally surrendered the country on May 5, 1945, just days before the end of the war.

TOP RIGHT: **Paratroopers get ready to jump from their plane behind enemy lines in Occupied Holland.**

MIDDLE RIGHT: **The Belgian Brigade, an independent infantry group formed in Britain, enter Brussels.**

RIGHT: **A soldier miraculously survives as a shell explodes right next to him at Arnhem.**

LEFT: **Allied paratroops deploy during Operation Market Garden.**

TOP LEFT: **British troops advance on Venray, a transport hub in the Netherlands.**

TOP RIGHT: **The British Second Army patrol through the Dutch town of Susteren.**

MIDDLE LEFT: **American troops help salvage possessions from homes set alight by the retreating Germans.**

ABOVE: **German prisoners watch as British tanks pour into Belgium.**

MIDDLE RIGHT: **A smiling Belgian woman accompanies a British soldier as he marches a group of captured Germans through Antwerp.**

BELOW: **British troops crawl from house to house through a Dutch village.**

DAILY MAIL SEPTEMBER 26, 1944

Arnhem front

Alexander Clifford, in a delayed cable, tells below the story of the first corridor battle.

The Germans have tried the obvious thing. They cut through our corridor behind us, and - if you like to put it that way - technically surrounded us.

The moment came at noon on Friday. It was a long time before anyone worked out exactly what happened. But the effective news was that German tanks and infantry were across our lines about 17 miles north of Eindhoven. All convoys must halt. The attack came from Germany itself. It may have been combined with an attempt to rescue some of the estimated 70,000 Germans who are partly cut off in Western Holland. Its main purpose was certainly to cut the axis.

From that moment the campaign abandoned all the rules again and became a series of personal adventures of each individual. For many truck drivers it meant sitting patiently by the roadside and listening to the firing ahead. For the men on the Arnhem front it meant the queer feeling that they were no longer fighting at the end of lines of supply but were temporarily in a military vacuum. For me it meant that I was cut off from my kit, which I had left in a little inn in the village where the Germans had attacked. It had been a gay, clean little inn, with an innkeeper who still managed to provide comfort and good Dutch food. And now the German mortars were falling on it.

Good humour

For the men on that section of the road it meant a sudden inferno of battle at a spot technically 30 miles behind our front lines. British and German trucks were blazing along the road and out into the fields. The possibility had been clearly enough foreseen. We always knew we could deal with anything of the sort if it occurred, and around Nijmegen there was a great deal of good-humoured banter as people who had been cut off began to go round trying to find billets for the night.

In the desert one would have joined some unit and slept in its laager. Here in civilised Europe one hardly knew what to do. In the end I and those with me decided to sleep on the billiards tables of a wayside pub. We ate sumptuously off German rations which we found in a train at Nijmegen railway station.

The night was a succession of wild alarms. Dutchmen, either honestly misinformed or deliberate Fifth Columnists, kept streaming in to tell us that the Germans were a mile away, that the British were evacuating Nijmegen, and so forth. None of it was remotely true. But the whole position was so unorthodox that it was understandable.

There was plenty of shooting during the night. But as often happens near the front, when morning came no one knew what it had been about. The only certain news was that the Germans were still across our path. Tanks had been sent to deal with them.

I followed down behind the leading patrol. It was necessary to reach that little inn quickly if any of my kit was to be saved. The Germans were reported to have been in the village itself for quite a few hours.

The ruptured stretch of axis was a trail of wrecked vehicles. It was almost like Normandy again, for the fields were strewn with dead cows. The tarmac was churned to dust where swerving tanks had ground it up. Half a dozen cottages along the way were still burning.

Methodical

While our patrol was still passing through all this we looked up and saw a new mighty phase of this three dimensional campaign. The sky filled fuller than I have ever seen it with planes and gliders. They came low, flying in steady and majestic patterns. They were simply reinforcements for the front. The Germans began to shoot at them. It was alarming to hear how near the Germans still were to the centre-line of our axis. They were firing from the nearest woods two fields away and their bullets were spangling the cloudy sky all round the great air fleet.

They got some hits. Extraordinarily few in the circumstances, but they could hardly help getting some. A towing plane began to burn and circled from the rest. Two or three gliders slipped loose and swung round towards what they knew were our lines.

But the Germans had given their positions away and firing broke out savagely once more from our land forces. A battle started chaotically among the fields and copses and farmhouses round about. It looked chaotic. But there was plenty of method in the way the Germans were being elbowed aside. You could piece it all together by watching the positions of the tanks along the roads and the places where the anti-tank guns were being dug in and the columns of smoke where our shells were falling.

And then we came to the gay, neat little village in whose inn we had left all our kit. Now it was empty and splintered and broken. It was grey with a pall of dust. Its streets were a tapestry of fallen branches and loose tiles and scattered bricks.

The inn itself was windowless and derelict. The innkeeper and his family were alive - they were down in the cellar steadfastly singing hymns. Almost everything they possessed was broken. Their yard was full of dead chickens. We dug what remained of our things out of the wreckage of our bedrooms. An American paratrooper came and told us to be quick about it, the village still wasn't very healthy.

L IS
R TIME
R FRENCH
TROOPS

ng hard for
bring up to
nd-infantry
reth Line to

Soviet advances in the east

The Soviet victory at Stalingrad in January 1943 marked a reversal of fortunes in the East. Within weeks the Red Army had liberated Kharkov and Kursk, but the Wehrmacht was not yet entirely on the defensive, and managed to recapture Kharkov one month later. In July 1943, Hitler launched an enormous offensive to retake Kursk and deal a resounding blow to the Red Army. 'Operation Citadel' as the attack was codenamed, was the largest tank battle in history, with more than 6,000 taking part in total. Despite suffering heavy losses, the Red Army won the battle and began an unrelenting march westward towards Berlin.

After Kursk, Soviet cities were liberated one after another; Kharkov was taken for the second time in August, followed by Smolensk in September and Kiev in November. The Soviet advance continued throughout early 1944, and by June, the Red Army had reached Belarus. Although the key to the Red Army's success was sheer manpower, it also benefited from a superior number of tanks and aircraft. Minsk fell on July 3 – along with 100,000 German prisoners – and by the end of the month they had advanced into eastern Poland. On October 1, with the Red Army just miles away, the residents of Warsaw rose up in rebellion against German rule. However, Stalin halted the Russian advance and left the fighters, who were largely anti-Communist, to their fate. German revenge was terrible and some 200,000 Poles died. When the Soviet Union did finally enter Warsaw in January 1945, it was far from the liberation that most Poles had hoped for.

Conspiracy against Hitler

With the Allies closing in on both fronts, it seemed that Germany's defeat might be within sight. This undoubtedly encouraged conspirators within the German Army to go ahead with plans to assassinate the Führer. With Germany standing on the edge of an abyss, some German generals, who had always been lukewarm about Nazism, believed peace should be made with the Western Allies so the Army could concentrate on keeping the Soviets from advancing on the Reich. One of the officers, Count von Stauffenberg, who was attached to Hitler's general staff, placed a bomb under a table at his headquarters in East Prussia on July 20, 1944. However, the bomb failed to kill Hitler and the conspirators were 'strung up like cattle' upon his orders.

The Siege of Leningrad

During the war Leningrad (St. Petersburg) was subjected to one of the longest sieges in modern history. The city was blocked-off by the German army from September 1941 until January 1943, during which time more than a million people died of starvation. The Soviets were able to get some supplies in and civilians out across Lake Ladoga, but convoys ran the gauntlet of German guns and millions remained trapped and starving inside the city. In January 1943, the Red Army launched Operation Iskra, a major offensive which punched a hole through the German siege lines within days. Fighting around the city continued for another year until the German Army was forced to retreat in January 1944.

DAILY MAIL JANUARY 19, 1943

Leningrad free

The siege of Leningrad, second city of Russia, which has been blockaded by the German armies for more than 16 months, has been raised. Russian troops storming across the Neva River have smashed through the enemy's mighty defence zone and advanced 45 miles.

This tremendous news was given to the world in a special Moscow communiqué last night. A second special communiqué announced equally momentous successes on the southern front. Here Russian troops have crossed both the Donetz and Manych rivers - last great natural barriers protecting Rostov. Today the road to Rostov lies open. Thousands more prisoners have been taken on both these fronts; more towns captured in the North Caucasus, and the encircled German army at Stalingrad split in two.

South of Voronezh the enemy are falling back, abandoning their equipment and large quantities of supplies. Over 1,000 motor vehicles were captured intact on one stretch of road.

Here are the texts from the communiqués: A few days ago our troops concentrated south of Lake Ladoga launched an offensive against the German Fascist troops besieging Leningrad. They were given the task of destroying the enemy defences and thereby lifting the siege of Leningrad. It must be borne in mind that during the many months of the siege of Leningrad the Germans converted their positions on the approaches to the city into a strongly fortified area consisting of concrete emplacements and other fortifications.

The offensive of our troops was launched from two directions - from the western bank of River Neva, south-west and south-east of Schluesselburg, and from the east from the area south of Lake Ladoga. Having breached the enemy's defences, which extended to a depth of about nine miles, and having crossed the Neva, our troops in the course of seven days of severe fighting occupies the town of Schluesselburg. They also seized the large fortified points of Maryino Moskovskaya-Dubrobskaya, and Lipka; eight workers settlements and the railway stations of Sinyavino and Podgornaya.

Thus, after the first battles, the troops of the Volkhov and Leningrad fronts joined up on January 18, and broke through the investment of Leningrad. According to incomplete data our troops took prisoner 1,261 officers and men. In the course of the battle our artillery and mortars destroyed 470 fortified centres and block-houses, 25 strongly equipped observation posts, and 172 artillery and mortar batteries were silenced.

The break-through was carried out partly by the forces of the Leningrad front commanded by General Govorov and partly by the forces of the Volkhov front commanded by Army General Meretskov. Co-ordination of action of troops on both fronts was achieved by the representatives of Supreme Headquarters. Marshals of the Soviet Union Zhukov and Voroshilov.

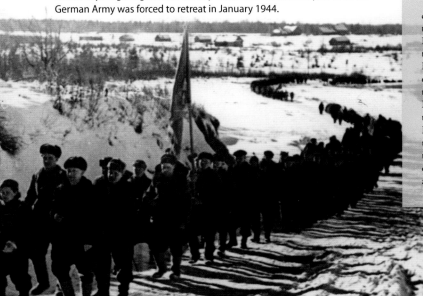

Island-hopping

After securing Guadalcanal and New Guinea in 1943 the Americans continued with their offensives in the Pacific, jumping from island to island, moving ever closer to Japan in a strategy known as 'island-hopping'. In the summer of 1944 the US liberated Saipan, Guam and Tinian in the Marianas Island chain, and the invasion of Peleliu and Angaur in the Palau island group followed shortly after. The capture of these islands helped put America's B-29 bombers within range of Japan's main island, and from June 1944 the US Army Air Force began a bombing campaign against Japanese cities with the intention of forcing the country into submission. In 1945 the bombing became relentless, especially in Tokyo, where thousands of people were killed in firebombing raids, but the Japanese government still refused to surrender.

TOP: **In September 1944, US troops wade ashore almost unopposed on Morotai, one of the Moluccas Islands in the Dutch East Indies.**

ABOVE LEFT: **Marines take cover as they meet with Japanese mortar fire on the beaches of Peleliu in the Palau island group.**

BELOW: **With the help of a jeep, US troops push an anti-tank gun ashore on the island of Angaur in the Palau group.**

ABOVE: **An American tank rolls through Garapan, the main city on Saipan island, after the Japanese had been pushed out in July 1944.**

LEFT: **A long line of amphibious tanks come ashore at Tinian Island in the Marianas chain, August 1944.**

Battle for the Philippines

The United States had shared a close relationship with the Philippines ever since the islands were ceded to Washington at the end of the Spanish-American War of 1898. Thousands of American troops were in the Philippines when the Japanese invaded within hours of the attack on Pearl Harbor. Many were captured and, together with Filipino POWs, they were forced to endure an infamous death march to their internment camp in Bataan. The battle to liberate the Philippines from Japanese rule began on October 20, 1944 when US troops under the command of General Douglas MacArthur landed on the island of Leyte. The Japanese attempted to obstruct the landings in what became the largest naval battle of the entire war. The US scored a decisive victory, neutralizing the Japanese Navy and allowing US and Australian forces to steadily recapture the Philippines. The Battle for Manila began in February 1945 and ended up being the only major urban battle fought in the Pacific campaign. Fighting was fierce and it took American soldiers more than one month to secure the city. By the time it fell on March 3, thousands of civilians had been killed and the city was almost utterly destroyed.

ABOVE: **An American soldier is carried by stretcher, past the bodies of dead Japanese soldiers, to a dressing station set up amid the debris of Manila City Hall.**

LEFT: **An aerial view of the devastation caused during the fight for Manila. It was to be the only major urban battle of the Pacific campaign.**

BELOW: **Plumes of smoke rise above Manila during fierce fighting between US and Japanese forces in February 1945.**

Hitler's last stand

Although the Allies had made great strides through France and Belgium, Hitler would not accept the inevitability of defeat. A fresh offensive was planned in the Ardennes where the Allied line was weakest and his new 'wonder' weapons were ready to rain down a new terror upon London.

Battle of the Bulge

The German Army launched its attack in the Ardennes in mid-December 1944. The plan was to split the Allied forces in two and create a corridor to the sea at Antwerp. The Allies managed to halt the advance on Antwerp, but not before it created a large bulge in the Allied line. The Wehrmacht found itself up against the might of the United States Army and Air Force and by January the attack had waned. The attack only served to delay the Allied invasion of Germany temporarily and came at a cost of thousands of German lives.

TOP: **Refugees flee from the Germans' December 1944 offensive in the Ardennes.**

ABOVE UPPER MIDDLE: **A small infantry group of the US 82nd Airborne ambush a German patrol near Bra in Belgium.**

ABOVE LOWER MIDDLE: **Allied troops cycle past damage done to the town of Bastogne during the German offensive.**

ABOVE: **The frozen body of a German soldier lies in the snow near Nefte. Many Germans questioned the** wisdom of the Ardennes offensive, which cost many lives and diverted resources from the Eastern Front.

ABOVE LEFT: **German soldiers lie dead in the snow after attempting to storm Allied positions at Bastogne in Belgium during the 'Battle of the Bulge'.**

LEFT: **Members of the US Third Army, under the command of General Patton, advance on Houffalize in Belgium.**

'Wonder weapons'

In addition to his offensive in the Ardennes, Hitler had placed his faith in a new generation of secret weapons that would, he believed, inflict devastating damage on Britain. The first of these was the V1, a pilotless flying bomb, which began falling on London and south-east England from June 1944. They caused casualties and heavy damage, as well as a dip in morale since most people had thought that the dangers of the Blitz had passed. They also somewhat helped Hitler reverse his rapidly declining popularity at home. Many Germans wanted retribution for the relentless Allied bombing campaign and Hitler's new weapon offered just that; the letter V was short for 'Vergeltung' the German word for revenge. The threat from the V1 decreased as the Allied troops overran the launch sites in northern France. Between June and early September, it is thought that almost 7,000 were launched; over half were destroyed before reaching their intended targets.

London came under attack from another German 'wonder' weapon, the V2, from September onwards. These, in contrast to the V1s, were long-range rockets and were fired from sites in places still controlled by the Nazis. The renewed threat from the skies revived the need to evacuate children from the vulnerable areas, and some 200,000 mothers and their children were forced to leave London. Nevertheless, Hitler's 'wonder weapons' were too little too late. Hitler had promised the German public great things from his 'wonder weapons', and when it became obvious that they would not alter the outcome of the war, the Nazis lost whatever public support they still had.

ABOVE: **A tragic image reveals the aftermath of a V2 attack on the Belgian coast.**

BELOW: **An anti-aircraft gun shoots down Hitler's 'wonder weapons' over Belgium.**

DAILY MAIL NOVEMBER 9, 1944

V2 Terror in London

Hour by hour last night Germany put out claims that V2 is causing widespread damage in London. Here, said radio spokesmen, was a long-range weapon more dangerous than V1. They said it had destroyed Euston Station, smashed a railway bridge, and devastated five named areas.

Goebbels seized on V2 as a morale builder to replace the anniversary celebrations of the Munich beer cellar putsch, abandoned this year for the first time.

The weapon - neutral sources have described it as a rocket-shell 'like a flying telegraph pole with a trail of flame behind it' - was said to have been in use for some weeks. But Berlin made no mention of it until yesterday.

First came a brief reference in the High Command's communiqué and then a spate of boosting radio reports and commentaries. Among all the claims there was one significant admission - that the launching of the 'deadly weapon' caused sacrifices 'among the crews.'

The Germans claimed to be in possession of full information of the damage caused by V2. 'The British Government,' said one radio spokesman, 'has so far concealed from its people that a more effective, more telling, and therefore more dangerous long-range weapon has been in action in addition to the so-called flying bomb, which everyone knows about now.

'The German Command possess exact reports on the success and the effect of V2. If they required further proof of its accuracy, official British reports have supplied it by announcing, after nights in which London was exclusively attacked with V2, that flying bombs had again been over the capital.

'For the time being nothing further can be made known about the technical details of this missile. According to reports from England, the characteristic feature of the new weapon is that it cannot be heard or seen before its extraordinarily heavy detonation.'

Reports from Sweden and other neutral countries have credited V2 with a range of between 200 and 300 miles and a warhead of something under a ton of high explosive. Bases in Germany, Holland, Denmark, and Norway have been claimed as feasible for attacks on Britain. A rocket, it is said, would have to rise some 50 miles into the sky to achieve any considerable range, and it would travel at well over 700 miles per hour.

ROCKETS—NOW IT CAN BE TOLD
1,200 Fell; Essex Worst Blitzed; Deptford Worst Incident

THIS PAGE & OPPOSITE: **This extraordinary sequence of photographs captures the chaos in the minutes following the devastating explosion of the V2 that fell on Smithfield, London.** In the picture sequence opposite, traders and other civilians work with police and ARP to release a casualty but it's clear there was nothing that could be done for this unnamed victim.
The images on this page show the ironwork forming the roof and facade of the handsome Victorian building twisted beyond recognition and tangled in the rubble, causing complications for the heavy rescue squad seen at work with a crane (this page top).

Smithfield Market destroyed

One of the worst V2 incidents of the Blitz was the devastation of Smithfield, London's historic meat and poultry market – an extensive enclosed indoor market at the corner of Farringdon Street and Charterhouse Street where the rocket landed. At 11.10 am it was filled with buyers and sellers, while others were queuing outside to get in. The V2 fell out of the sky virtually destroying the crowded building, its blast making a crater that penetrated the railway tunnel and extensive sidings running below; the casualties, commodities and rubble mingled in a horrible melée. The decorative ironwork that formed the intricate facade collapsed in a tangle, making rescue work even more difficult. One hundred and ten people died immediately from the blast and many more were seriously injured.

Iwo Jima

On February 19, 1945 the 3rd, 4th and 5th divisions of the United States Marine Corps staged an amphibious invasion of Iwo Jima, an island some 700 miles south of Tokyo. The fighting was among the fiercest in the Pacific theatre, costing almost 7,000 American lives, making it the deadliest battle in the history of the US Marines. Countless more Japanese died as they defended the island to the death, first engaging the marines in the open and later resisting from hiding places in caves. The battle ended on March 26, by which time 27 American servicemen had performed acts of bravery that would win them the Medal of Honor.

TOP: The marines move up the beach under the shadow of the extinct volcano, Mount Suribachi.

ABOVE: Marines of the 4th Division storm the shores of Iwo Jima.

BELOW LEFT: An aerial view of the American invasion force approaching the shore of Iwo Jima, February 19, 1945.

BELOW RIGHT: The American flag is raised on Mount Suribachi on February 23, 1945.

OPPOSITE LEFT: Two marines kneel to pray in their fox holes in a rare quiet moment during the Iwo Jima campaign.

OPPOSITE TOP RIGHT: US marines attempt to flush Japanese soldiers out of a cave on Okinawa.

OPPOSITE MIDDLE RIGHT: Marines brace themselves as they detonate a satchel charge in a cave used by the Japanese to attack their positions on Okinawa.

OPPOSITE BELOW RIGHT: After capturing the Marianas islands in 1944, the US established several large military

bases from where B-29 Superfortress bombers could attack the Japanese home islands.

OPPOSITE BOTTOM: The cemetery of the 5th Marine Division on Iwo Jima. Almost 7,000

American servicemen lost their lives in the battle for the island.

200 TANKS "LAND ON IWO JIMA"

TERRIFIC BATTLE AS U.S. MARINES PUSH ON

U.S. Marines are fighting a "terrific battle" on the Japanese outpost fortress of Iwo Jima, said a U.S. radio commentator at Admiral Nimitz's advanced H.Q. to-day.

The Americans, within 24 hours of landing, have already put about 200 tanks ashore, said a Tokio broadcast.

Another landing was made to-day, covered by constant air and sea bombardment, and there are now 20,000 Marines ashore, added Tokio.

Mazed Defences

The Marines are fighting their way across the island through a maze of pillboxes, blockhouses, and positions threaded with miles of trenches.

"It is a tough job, and nobody underestimates the strength of positions which the Japanese have fortified for years," cabled Reuter's special correspondent in the flag-ship.

Large fires were left burning in

Okinawa

In mid-March as the Battle for Iwo Jima was drawing to a close, the US began the next offensive against the island of Okinawa. At just over 300 miles from Kyushu, the southernmost of Japan's four main islands, Okinawa was to be a springboard for the invasion of Japan proper. After a week long 'softening up' bombardment from the air, US troops of the Tenth Army came ashore largely unopposed. However, the Japanese were lying in wait at better-defended locations and the battle soon became a bloodbath. It took the US almost three months to wrestle control of the island and defeat the Japanese, who once again fought to the death. Unlike Iwo Jima, Okinawa had a large civilian population, which had been warned by Japanese propaganda not to expect any mercy from the Americans. Such scaremongering had terrible consequences; thousands of civilians committed suicide and thousands more died in the fighting. By the end of the battle an estimated 100,000 Japanese and 12,000 American servicemen had lost their lives.

FIFTH MARINE DIVISION

Advancing through Germany

The early months of 1945 saw events moving fast, as the German will to fight on began to diminish. Throughout January the Russian Armies advanced remorselessly upon the country from the east, liberating the Nazi concentration camp at Auschwitz on January 27. By now it was obvious to almost everyone involved that the final defeat of Germany was inevitable and imminent and Roosevelt, Churchill and Stalin met at Yalta in the Crimea between February 4–11 to discuss the post-war division of Germany.

On April 14, the Red Army took Vienna and then turned its attention towards Berlin. The Russians crossed the Oder and two armies encircled Berlin on April 25. They joined to the west and then turned back towards the semi-ruined city, now devastated by artillery bombardment as well as by heavy bombing. Meanwhile the Allies were pushing on to the Rhineland and American troops captured the bridge at Remagen intact on March 7, at last establishing a much-needed bridgehead across the Rhine. Other Allied crossings were made and their forces now moved much further into Germany. American troops were just 60 miles from Berlin by 12 April.

TOP: **Stalin and Roosevelt discuss the post-war settlement in Europe at the Yalta Conference in February 1945.**

MIDDLE RIGHT: **Russian POWs show their gratitude to one of the American GIs who liberated their prison camp.**

ABOVE: **Civilians in the German city of Rheydt, birthplace of Joseph Goebbels, cautiously emerge with white flags as the Americans approach.**

ABOVE LEFT: **American and Soviet troops link up for the first time at Torgau on the River Elbe on April 25, 1945.**

BELOW: **While bridges were being constructed across the Rhine, thousands of paratroops were dropped into Germany by the largest airborne fleet ever assembled for a single mission. German civilians watch in amazement as the fleet, stretching some 500 miles, passes overhead.**

300,000 TROOPS OVER THE RHINE
"1st" and "3rd" Linking: Patton Eating Up Territory: Essen 9 Miles: Monty Brushes the Panzers Aside

The West Front Jig-saw To-day

NAZIS

ROLLING OVER THE RHINE goes the non-stop stream of Allied transport.

DAILY MAIL MARCH 9, 1945

The Rhine crossed

We've done it. Early this morning strong infantry forces of General Hodge's American First Army are streaming across the Rhine into our newly won bridgehead on the east bank of the river. The final drive to meet the Russian armies in the heart of Germany - the last heave to end the war - has begun.

You can throw your hats in the air to-day. The success of our lightning stroke undoubtedly shortens the war by months. We are massing substantial forces in our rapidly expanding bridgehead 290 miles from Berlin.

This historic moment in the war came at 4.30 p.m. on Wednesday, when a spearhead task force of the First Army crossed the river in a sudden thrust which took the Germans completely by surprise. The crossing was made between Bonn and Coblenz. Opposition was light. Once on the other side the Americans spread out to get elbow-room. Then our main forces poured over. Before their tremendous onslaught the German defences cracked - then collapsed like a pack of cards.

More and more men swarmed across the river, and swiftly, efficiently, the bridgehead was built up.

TOP LEFT: **A fourteen-year-old boy is taken prisoner by the Allies. As the Allies closed in, Hitler futilely ordered that children help defend the Reich.**

TOP MIDDLE: **British troops pass the bodies of dead Germans as they move along the eastern bank of the Rhine.**

TOP RIGHT: **Russian soldiers advance across open fields in Germany.**

ABOVE: **Winston Churchill and General Montgomery cross the Rhine with American troops.**

BELOW: **As the German Army retreated from the advancing Allies, they destroyed most of the bridges across the Rhine. Engineers had to build makeshift bridges so the Allies could cross into Germany.**

YOU ARE NOW CROSSING THE RHINE RIVER THROUGH COURTESY OF E CO. 17 ARMD. ENGR. BN. AND C CO. 202 ENGR. C. BN.

PORTED OVER ELBE,
BERLIN DEFENCES

Busmen GIRL "SAVED"

Germans Never Fired That Gun

DAILY MAIL MAY 3, 1945

Italy, Austria and Berlin fall with 1,000,000 prisoners

The Wehrmacht has collapsed. Berlin has fallen. Hitler and Goebbels are now reported to have killed themselves in the dying capital.

The German armies - 1,000,000 men - in Northern Italy and Western Austria have surrendered unconditionally. The Southern Redoubt has been torn to pieces. And, according to San Francisco reports, surrender in Holland, Denmark and Norway is expected at any hour.

These are the highlights of the war news this morning as Germany totters to complete defeat. Surrender of the shattered remnants of Berlin's garrison was announced in an Order of the Day by Marshal Stalin to Marshals Zhukov and Koniev. The end came at three o'clock yesterday afternoon. By nine o'clock 70,000 German prisoners had been counted.

It was left to General Webling, an obscure artillery commander, to give up the keys of Berlin to the Russians after 11 days' fighting. Stalin's Order described Hitler's former capital as "the centre of German aggression and cradle of German imperialism."

Surrender of the German armies in Italy and Western Austria was announced by Mr. Churchill to a cheering House of Commons. President Truman, giving the news in Washington, said: "Only folly and chaos can now delay the general capitulation of the everywhere-defeated German armies."

In Northern Germany the whole pocket covering the North Sea ports and Denmark is swiftly collapsing. Germans running blindly from the Russians are being swamped. Denmark is cut off. British troops have raced 50 miles across its southern approaches, captured Lübeck, and swept beyond to another Baltic port - Wismar.

Montgomery's British and American forces are storming forward on a 40-miles front to meet Rokossovsky's army. The Russians are less than 28 miles away after seizing Rostock, on the Baltic, and a number of other towns to the south.

Civilians in chaos

Roads leading from the Lübeck area towards Denmark are an inferno of destruction. British planes, swooping on the fleeing Germans, have smashed more than 1,000 lorries. For miles the highways are cluttered with burning German transport mingled with frantic civilian refugees.

An hour before announcing the fall of Rostock last night, Marshal Stalin reported that the big German pocket south-east of Berlin has crumbled. The Russians captured more than 120,000 Germans.

In the doomed Southern Redoubt, Patton's tanks are closing on the ruins of Hitler's Berchtesgaden "fortress." Swarming into Austria, other Third Army forces are 16 miles from Lina - about 70 miles from the Russians beyond Vienna.

News of the military position in Western Holland is obscure. But food is now pouring in to the hungry Dutch by land and air with full German agreement.

They quibble to the end.

The Holocaust

The Nazi regime subscribed to the belief that the German people sat atop of a global racial hierarchy and that other races – particularly Jews but also Gypsies and Slavs – were inferior and a threat to German racial purity. After they came to power in 1933, the Nazis began an incremental process of government-sponsored persecution against the country's Jewish population. They passed laws to deny Jews citizenship, to forbid them from marrying Aryans and to force them out of their jobs and businesses. The night of November 9, 1938, 'Kristallnacht', witnessed the first coordinated nationwide attack against Jews; many of Germany's synagogues were damaged and people were rounded up and sent to concentration camps. The following year, the war intervened and Germany's treatment of the Jews took an even deadlier turn.

ABOVE RIGHT: Polish Jews are rounded up in Warsaw and marched to a concentration camp in March 1940.

MIDDLE RIGHT: German soldiers massacre Jews in newly occupied Poland in retaliation for the death of a German soldier.

BELOW RIGHT: The Warsaw Ghetto burns as the Nazis try to suppress the uprising in April 1943.

BELOW: British soldiers liberated Belsen concentration camp on April 15, 1945. Thousands of people were found still alive but threatened by typhus, typhoid and dysentery, which were running rampant in the camp.

Final Solution

From October 1939, as the Nazis consolidated their control of Poland, the country's large Jewish population was forced to live in walled-off ghettoes where thousands of people died of starvation and disease. After the invasion of the Soviet Union in June 1941, the Nazis began directly killing Jews using mobile killing units called 'Einsatzgruppen', which murdered more than one million men, women and children behind the German lines. In late 1941 the Nazis began constructing death camps and by early 1942 they had decided upon a 'Final Solution': the extermination of all the Jews of Europe. Millions of people were sent to death camps such as Auschwitz, Treblinka, Sobibor and Belzec, where they were murdered in specially designed gas chambers. The 'lucky ones' were sent to work camps, where they faced gruelling labour and death from disease, hunger and maltreatment. By 1945, as Allied soldiers closed in on the camps, thousands of inmates were moved by train or on forced 'death marches' to prevent them from being liberated and to prolong their suffering. By the time the war was over, more than six million Jews had lost their lives, an estimated two thirds of Europe's pre-war Jewish population.

In addition, the Nazis dehumanized, detained and murdered hundreds of thousands of other people deemed to be racially undesirable or politically unsound. These groups included gypsies, homosexuals and Communists, as well as people with physical or mental illnesses who were also subjected to forcible sterilizations as part of a campaign of so-called 'racial hygiene'.

TOP RIGHT:
A mountain of shoes belonging to the deceased inmates of Belsen are used for fuel.

MIDDLE RIGHT: **Josef Kramer, the 'Beast of Belsen', was the only senior officer remaining at the camp when it was liberated by the British. He was put on trial and hanged in December 1945.**

BELOW RIGHT:
A snapshot of life around a water pump in a Nazi concentration camp after its liberation.

BELOW: **During 1945 the full extent of Nazi atrocities was slowly realized. Here shallow graves have been discovered in woods ouside Luneburg, Germany. A train on its way to Belsen stopped** near the city and some prisoners were instructed to get out and bury those who had died in the overcrowded wagons during the journey. Those who dug the graves were shot dead by the guards and buried with the rest.

'GERMANY SURRENDERS'
Doenitz Announcement on German Radio This Afternoon
ALL BRITAIN AWAITS BROADCAST BY MR. CHURCHILL

A DMIRAL KARL DOENITZ, FUEHRER OF GERMANY HAS ORDERED THE UNCONDIT... GERMAN F...

tasks, I turn at this tragic moment of our ... ... German nation.
... fight of almost six years ... hardness. Germany has su... overwhelming power of ...

DAILY MAIL   MAY 9, 1945
VE Day - it's all over

London, dead from six until nine, suddenly broke into victory life last night. Suddenly, spontaneously, deliriously. The people of London, denied VE-Day officially, held their own jubilation. 'VE-Day may be tomorrow,' they said, 'but the war is over to-night.' Bonfires blazed from Piccadilly to Wapping.

The sky once lit by the glare of the blitz shone red with the Victory glow. The last trains departed from the West End unregarded. The pent-up spirits of the throng, the polyglot throng that is London in war-time, burst out, and by 11 o'clock the capital was ablaze with enthusiasm.

Processions formed up out of nowhere, disintegrating for no reason, to re-form somewhere else. Waving flags, marching in step, with linked arms or half-embraced, the people strode down the great thoroughfares - Piccadilly, Regent-street, the Mall, to the portals of Buckingham Palace.

They marched and counter-marched so as not to get too far from the centre. And from them, in harmony and discord, rose song. The songs of the last war, the songs of a century ago. The songs of the beginning of this war - 'Roll out the Barrel' and 'Tipperary'; 'Ilkla Moor' and 'Loch Lomond'; 'Bless 'em All' and 'Pack Up Your Troubles.'

ABOVE: **VE Day in Moscow.** Aircraft searchlights are used to light up the night sky.

RIGHT: **VE Day in London.** Thousands gather for celebrations in Trafalgar Square.

BELOW: **VE Day in New York.** Thousands of people pour into Times Square in celebration of Germany's unconditional surrender.

Victory in Europe

By mid-April 1945, Russian troops were fighting their way through Berlin street by street, heading towards the Reichstag. Hitler had ordered 'fanatic determination' from all Germans in the defence of Berlin. However, he retreated to his underground bunker on April 16 and began to lose his grip on reality. On April 30, after nominating Admiral Karl Doenitz as his successor and blaming the Jews for the war, Hitler and his new wife Eva Braun committed suicide. On the same day, above ground, the battle for Berlin was won and the Soviet flag fluttered atop the ruins of the Reichstag building. The following day Hitler's propaganda minister Joseph Goebbels and his wife supervised the deaths of their six children before killing themselves. The remains of the German armies now began to surrender and, on May 7, General Eisenhower formally accepted the unconditional surrender of Germany. VE Day was celebrated across the world the following day, but the world was not yet at peace.

TOP RIGHT: **Street parties were held in towns and villages across Britain. Five and a half years of war had taken its toll on the British public; shortages and rationing would continue for several years.**

MIDDLE RIGHT: **With Britain and America pounding the city from above, and the Soviets attacking on the ground, Berlin is left as a shell of its former self.**

BELOW RIGHT: **Revellers pile onto a van as it drives through the crowds in Parliament Square, London, on VE Day.**

ABOVE: **The Soviet Union holds its official victory parade in Red Square, Moscow, on June 24.**

BELOW: **The Reichstag, the symbolic heart of Berlin, lies in ruins after the war.**

1,500 PLANES BATTERING TOKIO

"Preparing for Invasion"—Admiral Nimitz

150 WARSHIPS
COVER ATTACK

LEAVE SHIPS
SAIL TO-DAY

Big Three Tackle "Get Europe Working" Plan

STALIN MAY BRING A
JAP PEACE OFFER

Churchill-Truman Talk

WEA
PERIOD
LONDO
Mode
ing-is
FURTH
rain
thund
local
stor
Lia
Sun et
5.8 a
3.9 a.

NS
ght
nts
17;
ack

Victory in Japan

While victory was being celebrated in Europe, the war against Japan was still raging, but here too the Allies were pushing steadily forward. British forces finally liberated Burma from Japanese control on August 2, 1945, and the American push through the Pacific was bringing US troops gradually closer to Japan.

Roosevelt had died suddenly on April 12 and the new President, Harry Truman, was confronted with the challenging task of winning the war in the Far East. In July 1945, America successfully tested the first nuclear device and it was up to Truman to decide whether this potentially devastating piece of military technology should be used in the Pacific theatre. Truman realized how costly an invasion of the Japanese mainland would be; he had been given a foretaste when an estimated 12,000 Americans died taking Okinawa Island in March. He was also aware that the Allies were exhausted and that many people had lost focus on the Pacific campaign amid the jubilation of the victory in Europe. In addition, the Soviet Union was preparing to declare war on Japan and Truman was keen to stem Stalin's influence in the region. All these considerations encouraged Truman to take the momentous decision to use the bomb.

BOTTOM: The scene as troops of the Australian Seventh Division, supported by American ships and aircraft, landed east of the Japanese-held Borneo port of Balikpapan, a great oil centre.

TOP RIGHT: A Japanese tank trap on the beach at Tarakan Island, off the east coast of Borneo, snares an Australian light tank. Aussie engineers of the 9th Australian Imperial Forces division try to free it with another tank. A landing craft in the background is made ready to disgorge its valuable cargo.

ABOVE CENTRE: Australian forces begin their seaborne landings on the island of Tarakan, Borneo on May 1, 1945. The invasion was well-executed, though there were problems in landing; the Allies had overwhelming numbers by comparison with the Japanese garrison as fierce resistance was expected. Tarakan's oilfields were strategically important and the Allies hoped to make good use of the island's airfield. This picture shows the effectiveness of the modified landing craft that were equipped with rockets; these vessels could deliver devastating barrages with

lightning speed, just before infantry landed. Pockets of Japanese soldiers held out until June 21.

ABOVE LEFT AND RIGHT: Irrawaddy rail-head town, Prome, was liberated after a sharp encounter with a few straggling Japanese who held on while the bulk of their troops in the district were wandering aimlessly and defeated around the wild countryside south of the town. Allied armoured vehicles on the road to Prome were held up by a river crossing.

BELOW: **Fort Drum, nicknamed the Concrete Battleship, was a defensive installation built on a tiny island in Manila Bay to cover its approaches and the US garrison of Corregidor. The heavily fortified installation bristled with guns and fought hard to resist the Japanese who took it in 1942. When Allied forces recaptured Corregidor in February 1945, Fort Drum remained in the control of the Japanese until April 13 when US forces approached, avoided its heavy guns and landed. A landing craft tanker was called into use and several thousand gallons of an inflammable mixture were poured into the ventilation system and TNT charges set, creating an explosive inferno that wrecked the fort and** killed its garrison. **In this remarkable photograph, taken by Acme War Pool Correspondent, Stanley Troutman, the landing craft can be seen in the foreground while infantry cover the engineers who are feeding the fuel into the vents and setting their charges.**

TOP LEFT: **While conflict subsided in the European and Mediterranean theatres of war, the Allies remained engaged in fierce and deadly combat with Japan in the Far East. Australian troops were fighting in the jungle of New Guinea under the most difficult conditions resulting in many casualties.**

MIDDLE LEFT: **Ready for emergency a Bren-gunner takes cover alongside the track of the Western Railway at Labuan Island, Borneo, to cover the advance of the 9th Division Infantry.**

BELOW LEFT: **Australian soldiers pass the corpse of a Japanese soldier killed in the gateway leading to a plantation property on Labuan Island, Borneo.**

TOP RIGHT: **A feature of the naval operations off the Sakashima Islands in support of the Okinawa landings was the Japanese suicide aircraft attack. Here, firefighters are busy on board one of HM carriers of the British Pacific Fleet after a Japanese suicide plane had crash landed on the flight deck.**

NAGASAKI ATOM-BOMBED

"Good Results," Say Crew: More Than One Bomb May Have Been Dropped: Red Army Advances Rapidly

JAP HINT OF 'IMPORTANT DEVELOPMENT' SHORTLY

Ultimate weapon unleashed on Japan

The Potsdam Declaration set out the terms for Japan's unconditional surrender. These were sent to the Japanese government by Truman, Churchill and China's President Chiang Kai-shek on July 26. The Japanese government adopted a policy of ignoring the ultimatum because it took away all Japanese sovereignty and reduced its territories as well as threatening the prosecution of those guilty of war crimes. The response was delivered indirectly by the Japanese Prime Minister in a press conference. The ultimatum was uncompromising in guaranteeing the total devastation of Japan if it did not surrender, but the Imperial forces had no knowledge of the atomic bomb and had already withstood strategic bombing that had destroyed vast areas of some of its cities; the military would rather fight to the death than surrender and leave the Emperor at the mercy of foreign powers.

LEFT: The Allied powers called time on the Japanese and sent three B 29 bombers, one of them the *Enola Gay*, equipped with the 'Little Boy' nuclear device to bomb Hiroshima on August 6, followed by 'Fat Man' dropped on Nagasaki on August 9. The world suddenly became acquainted with the awesome weapon that would dominate military and political reality for generations to come, symbolized by the terrifying mushroom cloud, photographed here over Nagasaki.

INSET LEFT: The casing of an atomic bomb of the same type as 'Fat Man', on display in the USA.

TOP: Directly under the Hiroshima hypocentre was a modern ferro-concrete building which was one of the few that remained standing after the blast. A dazed survivor wanders the scorched streets. In the months and years to come many of the survivors of the blast died from terrible burns and horrible radiation sickness.

ABOVE: Nagasaki razed to the ground.

DAILY MAIL   AUGUST 8, 1945

City of 300,000 vanishes

Hiroshima, Japanese city of 300,000 people, ceased to exist at 9.15 on Monday morning. While going about its business in the sunshine of a hot summer day, it vanished in a huge ball of fire and a cloud of boiling smoke - obliterated by the first atom bomb to be used in the history of world warfare.

Such is the electrifying report of the American crew of the Super-Fortress which dropped the bomb as a cataclysmic warning to the Japs to get out of the war or be destroyed. Hiroshima, the whole crew agreed, was blotted out by a flash more brilliant than the sun.

They told their astonishing story here at Guam to-day. The explosion, they said, was tremendous and awe-inspiring. The words 'Oh my God' burst from every man as they watched a whole city blasted into rubble. Although they were ten miles away from the catastrophe, they felt the concussion like a close explosion of A.A. fire.

The men had been told to expect a blinding flash. They wore special black goggles. Only three of them knew what type of bomb was being dropped. 'It was hard to believe what we saw.' That was how Col. Paul W. Tibbits, pilot of the Super-Fort, described the explosion.

He said: 'We dropped the bomb at exactly 9.15 a.m. and got out of the target area as quickly as possible to avoid the full effect of the explosion. We stayed in the target area two minutes. The smoke rose to a height of 40,000ft.

'Only Captain Parsons, the observer; Major Ferebee, the bombardier; and myself knew what was dropped. All the others knew was that it was a special weapon. We knew at once we had got to get the hell out of there. I made a sharp turn in less than half a minute to get broadside to the target.

'All of us in the plane felt the heat from the brilliant flash and the concussion from the blast. 'Nothing was visible where only minutes before there was the outline of a city, with its streets and buildings and piers clearly to be seen. 'Soon fires sprang up on the edge of the city, but the city itself was entirely obscured.'

JAPAN SURRENDERS

"We Will Accept Potsdam 'Unconditional' Terms—If The Emperor's Prerogatives As Ruler Are Not Prejudiced"

ANTI-QUEUE ARMY MARCH IN WEST END
No. 40 to Get

TOP RIGHT: **The trio of planes flying towards Hiroshima on August 6 was picked up by Japanese radar and judged to be a reconnaissance flight so no defensive measures were taken. At around 8.15 am, the Little Boy nuclear device exploded about 2,000 feet above the target area in central Hiroshima creating a blaze of light and a shock wave that killed an estimated 70,000 citizens instantly and demolished all of the traditionally constructed buildings in range. In the *Enola Gay*, co-pilot Robert Lewis asked the question that would be repeated around the world: 'My God, what have we done?'**

ABOVE RIGHT: **Both Hiroshima and Nagasaki, though they were important cities for military reasons, were relatively untouched by strategic bombing. Tokyo, pictured, was not so unscathed –fire-bombing had already destroyed vast areas of the capital. The Allies avoided fire-bombing Kyoto but many other Japanese cities such as Nagoya were also devastated, fire-bombs destroying the many wooden buildings, rich with Japan's cultural and religious heritage.**

RIGHT: **The devastated city of Tokyo is pictured from the heavily defended US embassy in September 1945.**

BELOW: **A selection of newspapers from across the United States during the week of the atomic bombings.**

The big three at Potsdam

The Potsdam Conference was held at Cecilienhof, the home of Crown Prince Wilhelm Hohenzollern, in Potsdam, Occupied Germany, from July 17 to August 2, 1945. Participants were the Soviet Union, the United Kingdom and the United States. The three nations were represented by Communist Party General Secretary Joseph Stalin, Winston Churchill and US President Harry S. Truman. They gathered to decide how to administer punishment to the defeated Nazi Germany, which had agreed to unconditional surrender nine weeks earlier, on May 8, 1945. The goals of the conference also included the establishment of post-war order, peace treaties issues, terms for Japan's surrender and countering the effects of war.

ABOVE LEFT: **A London policeman is held aloft by military men from the US and New Zealand in celebration of VJ Day.**

BELOW: **Service men and women celebrate in Piccadilly.**

TOP RIGHT: **Winston Churchill, Harry S. Truman and Joseph Stalin pictured at Potsdam in 1945.**

ABOVE: **This was the scene in Piccadilly at three o'clock in the morning. Celebrations for VJ Day were, if anything, even more unrestrained than** those for VE Day. It was the end to a war which for people in Britain had lasted just twenty days short of six years.

VICTORIOUS LONDONERS CALL FOR THEIR KING AND QUEEN

TO-DAY'S THE DAY:

HOW THEY REJOICED

HUGE CROWDS

All night Queues to Get

VJ Day celebrations

Victory in Japan was made official on August 15 and London came to a standstill as celebrations began in earnest. By coincidence, it was also the State Opening of Parliament and the King and Queen's horse-drawn carriage ride to Westminster turned into an impromptu victory parade. In Trafalgar Square a fountain became part of the victory celebrations.

ABOVE: **The Royal Family on the balcony at Buckingham Palace.**

BELOW LEFT: **Crowds gather in Trafalgar Square on VJ Day – everyone had their own way of celebrating!**

BELOW RIGHT: **General Eisenhower returns to a hero's welcome as crowds throng Broadway in New York City in the hope of seeing him.**

BOTTOM: **People join together in the London streets on August 11 as news of the defeat, if not surrender, of Japan filters through.**

Peace

At Potsdam the Allied leaders agreed that Germany would be disarmed, 'de-nazified' and divided into four zones of occupation, controlled by Britain, the United States, the Soviet Union and France.

A final peace agreement was never signed and the Second World War soon gave way to the Cold War. The erstwhile Allies could not agree on the post-war make-up of Europe because of the ideological gulf between them. In southern and western Europe, Britain and America promoted democracy, free trade and anti-Communism, while in eastern Europe, the Soviet Union imposed centrally planned economies and Communist governments. According to Winston Churchill an 'iron curtain' had descended across Europe.

In the Pacific theatre, a peace treaty was more forthcoming. Japan was placed under American military occupation from 1945 until 1952. In the early 1950s, the United States had to turn its attention to the war in Korea and sought a peace treaty with Japan. The Treaty of San Francisco was signed in September 1951, officially ending the War in the Pacific when it came into effect the following April.

ABOVE RIGHT: Japan signs its official surrender to the British in Burma on September 12, 1945.

RIGHT: On July 17, 1945, the three major Allied powers met at Potsdam in an attempt to sort out the details of the peace process in Europe. The handshake here is the first meeting of Prime Minister Churchill with Harry S. Truman, the new American President. Tragically, President Roosevelt had died unexpectedly on April 12, 1945, less than a month before Germany's unconditional surrender, and as Vice-President, Truman was sworn in.

ABOVE: Churchill meets British military commanders at Berlin airport when he arrives for the Potsdam Conference. The Conference continued until the end of July but by that time Churchill was no longer British Prime Minister. Immediately after the victory against Germany, the Coalition government he had led since 1940 was dissolved and a new election called. Churchill's Conservative Party suffered a shock defeat as Labour won a landslide victory in a country eager for change. The Labour Prime Minister, Clement Attlee, replaced Churchill at Potsdam.

BELOW: On a visit to Berlin Churchill rests in a chair that was said to have been in the bunker in which Hitler committed suicide.

RIGHT: When the Japanese signed the Allies' surrender terms aboard the USS *Missouri* in Tokyo Bay, HMS *Duke of York*, flagship of Admiral Sir Bruce Fraser, Commander-in-Chief of the British Pacific Fleet, was alongside. Here, the Japanese interpreter who accompanied the pilot is searched upon his arrival aboard HMS *Duke of York*.

The Emperor of Japan.

THESE ARE THE POTSDAM CONDITIONS

Japs must give up all conquests

These, in brief, were the terms of the Three-Power Potsdam declaration to Japan:

1. Japan is given a last chance to end the war;

2. We will use all our forces till Japan submits;

3. Germany's fate is a warning to Japan; now the forces that beat Germany are facing Japan;

4. Japan must overthrow her militarists;

5. These are our only terms. They must be accepted immediately;

6. The Japanese militarists' influence must be eradicated for ever;

7. Japan must be occupied;

8. Japanese sovereignty must be limited to the main home islands of Japan; and such other islands as we allow them;

9. The Japanese Army, disarmed, may return home;

10. The Jap people will not be punished, but the war criminals must face trial;

11. All war industries must be erased;

12. Our occupation armies are to be withdrawn as soon as these conditions are fulfilled and a free, democratic government has been established; and

13. We call on Japan to surrender now, or face complete and utter destruction.

FAR LEFT: **Private H. Salter,** being measured here, is the first man to claim a 'non-austerity discharge suit'. Austerity Regulations had come into effect in March 1942. Clothing styles which used valuable materials merely for show were not permitted; so double-breasted jackets, turn-ups on trousers and decorative buttons were banned. By the time Private Salter was ready for discharge the war was going well enough for the regulations to be relaxed. The clothing entitlement is outlined in the poster in this demobilization centre.

LEFT: **A happy Private Salter** with his complete 'demob' outfit.

BELOW FAR LEFT: **Being measured for a 'demob' suit.** Many men had been in service for the duration of the war and had not acquired any new civilian clothing for years.

BELOW LEFT AND BOTTOM: **Scenes like this were repeated for the thousands of service personnel returning to 'civvy street.'**

Demobilizing the armed forces

Nine million American men and women had enlisted in the United States Armed Forces during World War II. Following the Axis surrenders, troops were deployed to Japan and Germany to occupy the two defeated countries. Two years after World War II, the Army Air Forces separated from the Army to become the United States Air Force.

At the start of the Second World War the British Army comprised fewer than one million men, including reserves. The number of recruits grew steadily during the course of the conflict and by the end of the war there were almost 5 million men and women in the forces. Post-war demobilization was rapid and by 1948 the number employed in the services had dipped below one million.

TOP RIGHT: Sgt Arthur Freund receives his Honourable Discharge from the US Army, which gave him the thanks of a grateful nation, a substantial cash payment, a service badge for his jacket and his discharge papers. A grand total of 11 million service personnel would follow in his footsteps.

ABOVE LEFT: German prisoners of war attending a service at Somerton Parish Church near Bury St Edmunds, photographed at choir practice. They sing their hymns from pencilled carbon copies of a German book.

ABOVE RIGHT: The smiles of these recently demobilized men speak louder than words.

BELOW: Axis POWs are put to work by British forces running feeding centres.

Living in peace

The end of the war brought enormous relief to the many that survived in its shadow but left millions displaced, bereaved, wounded, scarred psychologically or awaiting release from prison or the serving of a sentence in the courts of justice assembled by the victors. Some German prisoners had been transported across the Atlantic to labour for the war effort; many of them were content to stay in the countries that had imprisoned them, knowing the deprivations in their native land.

The rubble of Berlin had to be cleared and the civilians of the city set about creating some order, but there was much suffering as the German economy was shattered, the people dazed and afraid of the occupying troops. Food was scarce in Germany and the typical ration for German civilians left many close to starving. However, those that were willing to work, particularly those involved in heavier duties such as construction, fared much better and were paid well enough to supplement their rations, while aiding the reconstruction of their cities.

RIGHT AND BELOW:
Berliners, mainly women, work in chain gangs to clear rubble from bomb sites.

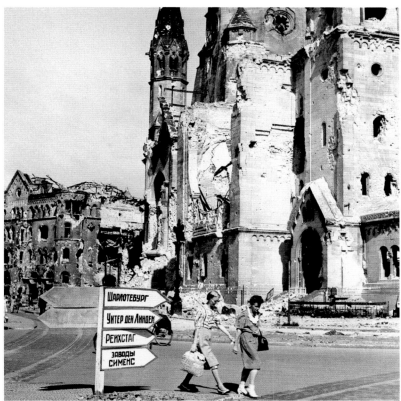

ABOVE LEFT: **On traffic duty at the Brandenburg Gate is a 22-year-old Russian woman soldier, Feodora Bondenko, who had marched from Kiev with Marshal Zhukov's forces.**

ABOVE RIGHT: **At a bend in the Kurfürstendamm, in front of the Kaiserin Augusta Gedächtniskirche, scarred by Allied bombing, two Berlin women pass by a Russian signpost.**

BELOW: **A crowd of Berliners wait for a bus in a street just off Potsdamer Platz. Buses were one of the few ways for citizens to get around the city but the service was severely curtailed. Life for the defeated citizens was harsh. They had to set about trying to clear up the wreckage, as rubble and damaged vehicles littered the streets. Food, clean water and shelter were all in short supply.**

The Nuremberg trials

Once the war was over, there was widespread agreement that the Nazi leaders should be brought to trial as war criminals. Some of them had escaped in the confusion of the final days of the war, and others, like Goebbels and Hitler himself, had avoided answering for their actions by committing suicide. Those who had been captured were brought before an International War Crimes Court. This met at Nuremberg in November 1945 and sat for several months, during which time it considered enormous amounts of evidence and heard very many witnesses. Of the 21 defendants, three were acquitted, seven received prison sentences ranging from ten years to life and the remainder were sentenced to death. The most notable among those to be executed were Field Marshal Göring and Joachim von Ribbentrop, the German Foreign Minister. Hours before he was due to be hung, Göring committed suicide by swallowing a cyanide capsule which he had managed to keep hidden, but on October 16, 1946, the executions of the others took place. Their bodies, together with that of Göring, were taken to Munich to be cremated and, according to the official announcement, their ashes were 'scattered in a river somewhere in Germany'.

ABOVE: **Rudolf Hess (left) and Joachim von Ribbentrop pictured during a mealtime at the Nuremberg courthouse.**

LEFT: **The defendants listen to the summing-up.**

BELOW: **Prisoners in the dock during the Nuremberg trials. Göring is on the far left.**

The world's biggest conflict

When the largest conflict the world had ever known finally came to an end, it had claimed the lives of an estimated 55 million people, the majority of whom were civilians. Some 20 million Russians, 10 million Chinese and 6 million European Jews, who were never part of the 100 million mobilized to fight, are believed to have perished. Modern warfare had been characterized by the employment of advanced technologies, which had led to the deaths of civilians across the globe, and had culminated in the use of the atomic bomb, the threat from which continues to overshadow our existence to this day.

LEFT: **Celebratory fireworks make a spectacular display in the night sky over the River Thames giving a suitable climax to Victory Day.**

BELOW: **On June 16, 1948, a ceremony took place in Cardiff as the remains of more than 4,000 American soldiers, most killed during the D-Day landings, were carried onboard the USS *Lawrence Victory* bound for New York.**